HILLS AND THE SEA

HILLS AND THE SEA

BY

HILAIRE BELLOC, M.P.

GREENWOOD PRESS, PUBLISHERS
WESTPORT, CONNECTICUT

Originally published in 1906
by Charles Scribner's Sons, New York

Reprinted from an original copy in the collections
of the Brooklyn Public Library

First Greenwood Reprinting 1970

Library of Congress Catalogue Card Number 71-109709

SBN 8371-4200-8

Printed in the United States of America

TO

THE OTHER MAN

CONTENTS

CONTENTS

MANY of these pages have appeared in the " Speaker,"
the " Pilot," the " Morning Post," the " Daily News,"
the " Pall Mall Magazine," the " Evening Standard,"
the "Morning Leader," and the "Westminster Gazette,"
to whose editors the author's best thanks are due for
the permission to reprint them.

THERE were once two men. They were men of might and breeding. They were young, they were intolerant, they were hale. Were there for humans as there is for dogs a tribunal to determine excellence; were there judges of anthropoidal points and juries to give prizes for manly race, vigour, and the rest, undoubtedly these two men would have gained the gold and the pewter medals. They were men absolute.

They loved each other like brothers, yet they quarrelled like Socialists. They loved each other because they had in common the bond of mankind; they quarrelled because they differed upon nearly all other things. The one was of the Faith, the other most certainly was not. The one sang loudly, the other sweetly. The one was stronger, the other more cunning. The one rode horses with a long stirrup, the other with a short. The one was indifferent to danger, the other forced himself at it. The one could write verse, the other was quite incapable thereof. The one could read and quote Theocritus, the other read and quoted himself alone. The high gods had given to one judgment, to the other valour; but to both that measure of misfortune which is their Gift to those whom they cherish.

From this last proceeded in them both a great knowledge of truth and a defence of it, to the tedium of their friends: a devotion to the beauty of women and of this world; an outspoken hatred of certain things and men, and, alas! a permanent sadness also. All these things the gods gave them in the day when the decision was taken upon Olympus that these two men should not profit by any great good except Friendship, and that all their lives through Necessity should jerk her bit between their teeth, and even at moments goad their honour.

The high gods, which are names only to the multitude, visited these men. Dionysius came to them with all his company once, at dawn, upon the Surrey hills, and drove them in his car from a suburb whose name I forget right out into the Weald. Pallas Athene taught them by word of mouth, and the Cytherean was their rosy, warm, unfailing friend. Apollo loved them. He bestowed upon them under his own hand the power not only of remembering all songs, but even of composing light airs of their own; and

Pan, who is hairy by nature and a lurking fellow afraid of others, was reconciled to their easy comradeship, and would accompany them into the mountains when they were remote from mankind. Upon these occasions he revealed to them the life of trees and the spirits that haunt the cataracts, so that they heard voices calling where no one else had ever heard them, and that they saw stones turned into animals and men.

Many things came to them in common. Once in the Hills, a thousand miles from home, when they had not seen men for a very long time, Dalua touched them with his wing, and they went mad for the space of thirty hours. It was by a stream in a profound gorge at evening and under a fretful moon. The next morning they lustrated themselves with water, and immediately they were healed.

At another time they took a rotten old leaky boat (they were poor and could afford no other)— they took, I say, a rotten old leaky boat whose tiller was loose and whose sails mouldy, and whose blocks were jammed and creaking, and whose rigging frayed, and they boldly set out together into the great North Sea.

It blew a capful, it blew half a gale, it blew a gale : little they cared, these sons of Ares, these

cousins of the broad daylight!   There were no
men on earth save these two who would not have
got her under a trysail and a rag of a storm-jib
with fifteen reefs and another: not so the heroes.
Not a stitch would they take in.   They carried all
her canvas, and cried out to the north-east wind:
" We know her better than you! She'll carry
away before she capsizes, and she'll burst long
before she'll carry away."   So they ran before it
largely till the bows were pressed right under, and
it was no human power that saved the gybe.   They
went tearing and foaming before it, singing a
Saga as befitted the place and time.   For it was
their habit to sing in every place its proper song—
in Italy a Ritornella, in Spain a Segeduilla, in
Provence a Pastourou, in Sussex a Glee, but on
the great North Sea a Saga.   And they rolled at
last into Orford Haven on the very tiptop of the
highest tide that ever has run since the Noachic
Deluge; and even so, as they crossed the bar they
heard the grating of the keel.   That night they
sacrificed oysters to Poseidon.

And when they slept the Sea Lady, the silver-
footed one, came up through the waves and kissed
them in their sleep; for she had seen no such men
since Achilles.   Then she went back through the
waves with all her Nereids around her to where

her throne is, beside her old father in the depths of the sea.

In their errantry they did great good. It was they that rescued Andromeda, though she lied, as a woman will, and gave the praise to her lover. It was they, also, who slew the Tarasque on his second appearance, when he came in a thunderstorm across the broad bridge of Beaucaire, all scaled in crimson and gold, forty foot long and twenty foot high, galloping like an angry dog and belching forth flames and smoke. They also hunted down the Bactrian Bear, who had claws like the horns of a cow, and of whom it is written in the Sacred Books of the East that:

> A Bear out of Bactria came,
> And he wandered all over the world,
> And his eyes were aglint and aflame,
> And the tip of his caudal was curled.

Oh ! they hunted him down and they cut him up, and they cured one of his hams and ate it, thereby acquiring something of his mighty spirit. . . . And they it was who caught the great Devil of Dax and tied him up and swinged him with an ash-plant till he swore that he would haunt the woods no more.

And here it is that you ask me for their names. Their names ! Their names? Why, they gave themselves a hundred names : now this, now that, but always names of power. Thus upon that great march of theirs from Gascony into Navarre, one, on the crest of the mountains, cut himself a huge staff and cried loudly :

"My name is URSUS, and this is my staff DREAD-NOUGHT : let the people in the Valley be afraid !"

Whereat the other cut himself a yet huger staff, and cried out in a yet louder voice :

"My name is TAURUS, and this is my staff CRACK-SKULL : let them tremble who live in the Dales !"

And when they had said this they strode shouting down the mountain-side and conquered the town of Elizondo, where they are worshipped as gods to this day. Their names? They gave themselves a hundred names !

"Well, well," you say to me then, "no matter about the names : what are names? The men themselves concern me ! . . . Tell me," you go on, "tell me where I am to find them in the flesh, and converse with them. I am in haste to see them with my own eyes."

It is useless to ask. They are dead. They will never again be heard upon the heaths at morning singing their happy songs : they will never more drink with their peers in the deep ingle-nooks of

home. They are perished. They have disappeared. Alas! The valiant fellows!

But lest some list of their proud deeds and
notable excursions should be lost on earth, and
turn perhaps into legend, or what is worse, fade
away unrecorded, this book has been got together ;
in which will be found now a sight they saw
together, and now a sight one saw by himself, and
now a sight seen only by the other. As also certain
thoughts and admirations which the second or
the first enjoyed, or both together : and indeed
many other towns, seas, places, mountains, rivers,
and men—whatever could be crammed between
the covers.

And there is an end of it.

HILLS AND THE SEA

THE NORTH SEA

IT was on or about a Tuesday (I speak without
boasting) that my companion and I crept in
by darkness to the unpleasant harbour of Lowestoft.
And I say "unpleasant" because, however charming for the large Colonial yacht, it is the very devil
for the little English craft that tries to lie there.
Great boats are moored in the Southern Basin,
each with two head ropes to a buoy, so that the
front of them makes a kind of entanglement such
as is used to defend the front of a position in warfare. Through this entanglement you are told to
creep as best you can, and if you cannot (who
could ?) a man comes off in a boat and moors you,
not head and stern, but, as it were, criss-cross, or
slant-ways, so that you are really foul of the next
berth alongside, and that in our case was a little
steamer.

Then when you protest that there may be a
collision at midnight, the man in the boat says

merrily, "Oh, the wind will keep you off," as though winds never changed or dropped.

I should like to see moorings done that way, at Cowes, say, or in Southampton Water. I should like to see a lot of craft laid head and tail to the wind with a yard between each, and, when Lord Isaacs protested, I should like to hear the harbour man say in a distant voice, "*Sic volo, sic jubeo*" (a classical quotation misquoted, as is the South-country way), "the wind never changes here."

Such as it was, there it was, and trusting in the wind and God's providence we lay criss-cross in Lowestoft South Basin. The Great Bear shuffled round the pole and streaks of wispy clouds lay out in heaven.

The next morning there was a jolly great breeze from the East, and my companion said, "Let us put out to sea." But before I go further, let me explain to you and to the whole world what vast courage and meaning underlay these simple words. In what were we to put to sea?

This little boat was but twenty-five feet over all. She had lived since 1864 in inland waters, mousing about rivers, and lying comfortably in mud-banks. She had a sprit seventeen foot outboard, and I appeal to the Trinity Brothers to explain what that means ; a sprit dangerous and horrible where there are waves ; a sprit that will catch every sea and wet the foot of your jib in the best of weathers ;

a sprit that weighs down already over-weighted bows and buries them with every plunge. *Quid dicam?* A Sprit of Erebus. And why had the boat such a sprit? Because her mast was so far aft, her forefoot so deep and narrow, her helm so insufficient, that but for this gigantic sprit she would never come round, and even as it was she hung in stays and had to have her weather jib-sheet hauled in for about five minutes before she would come round. So much for the sprit.

This is not all, nor nearly all. She had about six inches of free-board. She did not rise at the bows : not she ! Her mast was dependent upon a fore-stay (spliced) and was not stepped, but worked in a tabernacle. She was a hundred and two years old. Her counter was all but awash. Her helm —I will describe her helm. It waggled back and forth without effect unless you jerked it suddenly over. Then it "bit," as it were, into the rudder-post, and she just felt it — but only just — the ronyon !

She did not reef as you and I do by sane reefing points, but in a gimcrack fashion with a long lace, so that it took half an hour to take in sail. She had not a jib and foresail, but just one big head-sail as high as the peak, and if one wanted to shorten sail after the enormous labour of reefing the mainsail (which no man could do alone) one had to change jibs forward and put up a storm sail—under which (by the way) she was harder to put round than ever.

Did she leak? No, I think not. It is a pious opinion. I think she was tight under the composition, but above that and between wind and water she positively showed daylight. She was a basket. Glory be to God that such a boat should swim at all !

But she drew little water ? The devil she did ! There was a legend in the yard where she was built that she drew five feet four, but on a close examination of her (on the third time she was wrecked), I calculated with my companion that she drew little if anything under six feet. All this I say knowing well that I shall soon put her up for sale ; but that is neither here nor there. I shall not divulge her name.

So we put to sea, intending to run to Harwich. There was a strong flood down the coast, and the wind was to the north of north-east. But the wind was with the tide—to that you owe the lives of the two men and the lection of this delightful story ; for had the tide been against the wind and the water steep and mutinous, you would never have seen either of us again : indeed we should have trembled out of sight for ever.

The wind was with the tide, and in a following lump of a sea, without combers and with a rising glass, we valorously set out, and, missing the

South Pier by four inches, we occupied the deep.

For one short half-hour things went more or less well. I noted a white horse or two to windward, but my companion said it was only the sea breaking over the outer sands. She plunged a lot, but I flattered myself she was carrying Cæsar, and thought it no great harm. We had started without food, meaning to cook a breakfast when we were well outside : but men's plans are on the knees of the gods. The god called Æolus, that blows from the north-east of the world (you may see him on old maps—it is a pity they don't put him on the modern), said to his friends : " I see a little boat. It is long since I sank one"; and all together they gave chase, like Imperialists, to destroy what was infinitely weak.

I looked to windward and saw the sea tumbling, and a great number of white waves. My heart was still so high that I gave them the names of the waves in the eighteenth *Iliad* : The long-haired wave, the graceful wave, the wave that breaks on an island a long way off, the sandy wave, the wave before us, the wave that brings good tidings. But they were in no mood for poetry. They began to be great, angry, roaring waves, like the chiefs of charging clans, and though I tried to keep up my courage with an excellent song by Mr. Newbolt, "Slung between the round shot in Nombre

Dios Bay," I soon found it useless, and pinned my soul to the tiller. Every sea following caught my helm and battered it. I hung on like a stout gentleman, and prayed to the seven gods of the land. My companion said things were no worse than when we started. God forgive him the courageous lie. The wind and the sea rose.

It was about opposite Southwold that the danger became intolerable, and that I thought it could only end one way. Which way? The way out, my honest Jingoes, which you are more afraid of than of anything else in the world. We ran before it ; we were already over-canvased, and she buried her nose every time, so that I feared I should next be cold in the water, seeing England from the top of a wave. Every time she rose the jib let out a hundredweight of sea water ; the sprit buckled and cracked, and I looked at the splice in the forestay to see if it yet held. I looked a thousand times, and a thousand times the honest splice that I had poked together in a pleasant shelter under Bungay Woods (in the old times of peace, before ever the sons of the Achaians came to the land) stood the strain. The sea roared over the fore-peak, and gurgled out of the scuppers, and still we held on. Till (Æolus blowing much more loudly, and, what you may think a lie, singing through the rigging, though we were before the wind) opposite Alde-burgh I thought she could not bear it any more.

I turned to my companion and said : " Let us drive her for the shore and have done with it ; she cannot live in this. We will jump when she touches." But he, having a chest of oak, and being bound three times with brass, said : " Drive her through it. *It is not often we have such a fair wind.*" With these words he went below ; I hung on for Orfordness. The people on the strand at Aldeburgh saw us. An old man desired to put out in a boat to our aid. He danced with fear. The scene still stands in their hollow minds.

As Orfordness came near, the seas that had hitherto followed like giants in battle now took to a mad scrimmage. They leapt pyramidically, they heaved up horribly under her ; she hardly obeyed her helm, and even in that gale her canvas flapped in the troughs. Then in despair I prayed to the boat itself (since nothing else could hear me), "Oh, Boat," for so I was taught the vocative, " bear me safe round this corner, and I will scatter wine over your decks." She heard me and rounded the point, and so terrified was I that (believe me if you will) I had not even the soul to remember how ridiculous and laughable it was that sailors should call this Cape of Storms "the Onion."

Once round it, for some reason I will not explain, but that I believe connected with my prayer, the sea grew tolerable. It still came onto the land (we could sail with the wind starboard), and the wind blew harder yet ; but we ran before it more easily, because the water was less steep.   We were racing down the long drear shingle bank of Orford, past what they call "the life-boat house" on the chart (there is no life-boat there, nor ever was), past the look-out of the coastguard, till we saw white water breaking on the bar of the Alde.

Then I said to my companion, "There are, I know, two mouths to this harbour, a northern and a southern ; which shall we take?"   But he said, "Take the nearest."

I then, reciting my firm beliefs and remembering my religion, ran for the white water.   Before I knew well that she was round, the sea was yellow like a pond, the waves no longer heaved, but raced and broke as they do upon a beach.   One greener, kindly and roaring, a messenger of the gale grown friendly after its play with us, took us up on its crest and ran us into the deep and calm beyond the bar, but as we crossed, the gravel ground beneath our keel.   So the boat made harbour.   Then, without hesitation, she cast herself upon the mud, and I, sitting at the tiller, my companion ashore, and pushing at her inordinate sprit, but both revelling in safety, we gave thanks and praise.   That night we scattered her decks with wine as I had promised, and lay easy in deep water within.

But which of you who talk so loudly about the

island race and the command of the sea have had such a day? I say to you all it does not make one boastful, but fills one with humility and right vision. Go out some day and run before it in a gale. You will talk less and think more; I dislike the memory of your faces. I have written for your correction. Read less, good people, and sail more; and above all, leave us in peace.

THE SINGER

THE other day as I was taking my pleasure along a river called "The River of Gold," from which one can faintly see the enormous mountains which shut off Spain from Europe, as I walked, I say, along the Maille, or ordered and planted quay of the town, I heard, a long way off, a man singing. His singing was of that very deep and vibrating kind which Gascons take for natural singing, and which makes one think of hollow metal and of well-tuned bells, for it sounds through the air in waves; the further it is the more it booms, and it occupies the whole place in which it rises. There is no other singing like it in the world. He was too far off for any words to be heard, and I confess I was too occupied in listening to the sound of the music to turn round at first and notice who it was that sang; but as he gradually approached between the houses towards the river upon that happy summer morning, I left the sight of the houses, and myself sauntered nearer to him to learn more about him and his song.

I saw a man of fifty or thereabouts, not a mountaineer, but a man of the plains—tall and square, large and full of travel. His face was brown like chestnut wood, his eyes were grey but ardent; his brows were fierce, strong, and of the colour of shining metal, half way between iron and silver. He bore himself as though he were still well able to wrestle with younger men in the fairs, and his step, though extremely slow (for he was intent upon his song), was determined as it was deliberate. I came yet nearer and saw that he carried a few pots and pans and also a kind of kit in a bag: in his right hand was a long and polished staff of ashwood, shod with iron; and still as he went he sang. The song now rose nearer me and more loud, and at last I could distinguish the words, which were, in English, these:

"Men that cook in copper know well how difficult is the cleaning of copper. All cooking is a double labour unless the copper is properly tinned."

This couplet rhymed well in the tongue he used, which was not Languedoc nor even Béarnais, but ordinary French of the north, well chosen, rhythmical and sure. When he had sung this couplet once, glancing, as he sang it, nobly upwards to the left and the right at the people in their houses, he paused a little, set down his kit and his pots and his pans, and leant upon his stick to rest. A man in white clothes with a white square cap on his head ran out of a neighbouring door and gave him a saucepan, which he accepted with a solemn salute, and then, as though invigorated by such good fortune, he lifted his burdens again and made a dignified progress of some few steps forward, nearer to the place in which I stood. He halted again and resumed his song.

It had a quality in it which savoured at once of the pathetic and of the steadfast: its few notes recalled to me those classical themes which conceal something of dreadful fate and of necessity, but are yet instinct with dignity and with the majestic purpose of the human will, and Athens would have envied such a song.   The words were these:

"All kinds of game, Izard, Quails and Wild Pigeon, are best roasted upon a spit; but what spit is so clean and fresh as a spit that has been newly tinned?"

When he had sung this verse by way of challenge to the world, he halted once more and mopped his face with a great handkerchief, waiting, perhaps, for a spit to be brought; but none came.   The spits of the town were new, and though the people loved his singing, yet they were of too active and sensible a kind to waste pence for nothing.   When he saw that spits were not forthcoming he lifted up his kit again and changed his subject just by so much as might attract another sort of need.   He sang—but now more violently, and as though with a worthy protest :   Le lièvre et le lapin,
Quand c'est bien cuit, ça fait du bien.

That is: "Hare and rabbit, properly cooked,

do one great good," and then added after the necessary pause and with a gesture half of offering and half of disdain : "But who can call them well cooked if the tinning of the pot has been neglected?" And into this last phrase he added notes which hinted of sadness and of disillusion. It was very fine.

As he was now quite near me and ready, through the slackness of trade, to enter into a conversation, I came quite close and said to him, "I wish you good day," to which he answered, "And I to you and the company," though there was no company.

Then I said, "You sing and so advertise your trade?"

He answered, "I do. It lifts the heart, it shortens the way, it attracts the attention of the citizens, it guarantees good work."

"In what way," said I, "does it guarantee good work?"

"The man," he answered, "who sings loudly, clearly, and well, is a man in good health. He is master of himself. He is strict and well-managed. When people hear him they say, 'Here is a prompt, ready and serviceable man. He is not afraid. There is no rudeness in him. He is urbane, swift and to the point. There is method in this fellow.' All these things may be in the man who does not sing, but singing makes them apparent. Therefore in our trade we sing."

" But there must be some," I said, " who do not sing and who yet are good tinners."

At this he gave a little shrug of his shoulders and spread down his hands slightly but imperatively. " There are such," said he. " They are even numerous. But while they get less trade they are also less happy men. For I would have you note (saving your respect and that of the company) that this singing has a quality. It does good within as well as without. It pleases the singer in his very self as well as brings him work and clients."

Then I said, " You are right, and I wish to God I had something to tin ; let me however tell you something in place of the trade I cannot offer you. All things are trine, as you have heard " (here he nodded), " and your singing does, therefore, not a double but a triple good. For it gives you pleasure within, it brings in trade and content from others, and it delights the world around you. It is an admirable thing."

When he heard this he was very pleased. He took off his enormous hat, which was of straw and as big as a wheel, and said, " Sir, to the next meeting ! " and went off singing with a happier and more triumphant note, " Carrots, onions, lentils, and beans, depend upon the tinner for their worth to mankind."

ON "MAILLES"

A "MAILLE" is a place set with trees in
regular order so as to form alleys; sand and
gravel are laid on the earth beneath the trees,
masonry of great solidity, grey, and exquisitely
worked, surround the whole except on one side,
where strong stone pillars carry heavy chains
across the entrance. A "Maille" takes about two
hundred years to mature, remains in perfection for
about a hundred more, and then, for all I know,
begins to go off. But neither the exact moment
at which it fails nor the length of its decline is
yet fixed, for all "Mailles" date from the seventeenth century at earliest, and the time when most
were constructed was that of Charles II's youth
and Louis XIV's maturity—or am I wrong?
Were these two men not much of an age?

I am far from books; I am up in the Pyrenees.
Let me consider dates and reconstruct my formula.
I take it that Charles II was more than a boy
when Worcester was fought and when he drank
that glass of ale at Houghton, at the "George
and Dragon" there, and crept along under the
Downs to Bramber and so to Shoreham, where he

took ship and was free. I take it, therefore, that when he came back in 1660 he must have been in the thirties, more or less, but how far in the thirties I dare not affirm.

Now, in 1659, the year before Charles II came back, Mazarin signed the treaty with Spain. At that time Louis XIV must have been quite a young man. Again, he died about thirty years after Charles II, and he was seventy something when he died.

I am increasingly certain that Charles II was older than Louis XIV. . . . I affirm it. I feel no hesitation. . . .

Lord! How dependent is mortal man upon books of reference! An editor or a minister of the Crown with books of reference at his elbow will seem more learned than Erasmus himself in the wilds. But let any man who reads this (and I am certain five out of six have books of reference by them as they read), I say, let any man who reads this ask himself whether he would rather be where he is, in London, on this August day (for it is August) or where I am, which is up in Los Altos, the very high Pyrenees, far from every sort of derivative and secondary thing and close to all things primary?

I will describe this place. It is a forest of beech and pine; it grows upon a mountain-side so steep that only here and there is there a ledge on which

to camp. Great precipices of limestone diversify
the wood and show through the trees, tall and
white beyond them. One has to pick one's way
very carefully along the steep from one night's
camp to another, and often one spends whole
hours seeking up and down to turn a face of rock
one cannot cross.

It seems dead silent. There are few birds, and
even at dawn one only hears a twittering here and
there. Swirls of cloud form and pass beneath one
in the gorge and hurry up the opposing face of the
ravine ; they add to this impression of silence : and
the awful height of the pines and the utter remote-
ness from men in some way enhance it. Yet,
though it seems dead silent, it is not really so, and
if you were suddenly put here from the midst
of London, you would be confused by a noise
which we who know the place continually forget—
and that is the waterfalls.

All the way down the gorge for miles, sawing
its, cut in sheer surfaces through the rock, crashes
a violent stream, and all the valley is full of its
thunder. But it is so continuous, so sedulous,
that it becomes part of oneself. One does not lose
it at night as one falls asleep, nor does one recover
it in the morning, when dreams are disturbed by
a little stir of life in the undergrowth and one
opens one's eyes to see above one the bronze of the
dawn.

It possesses one, does this noise of the torrent, and when, after many days in such a wood, I pick my way back by marks I know to a ford, and thence to an old shelter long abandoned, and thence to the faint beginnings of a path, and thence to the high road and so to men ; when I come down into the plains I shall miss the torrent and feel ill at ease, hardly knowing what I miss, and I shall recall Los Altos, the high places, and remember nothing but their loneliness and silence.

I shall saunter in one of the towns of the plain, St. Girons or another, along the riverside and under the lime trees . . . which reminds me of "Mailles"! Little pen, little fountain pen, little vagulous, blandulous pen, companion and friend, whither have you led me, and why cannot you learn the plodding of your trade ?

THE PYRENEAN HIVE

SHUT in between two of the greatest hills in Europe—hills almost as high as Etna, and covering with their huge bases half a county of land—there lies, in the Spanish Pyrenees, a little town. It has been mentioned in books very rarely, and visited perhaps more rarely. Of three men whom in my life I have heard speak its name, two only had written of it, and but one had seen it. Yet to see it is to learn a hundred things.

There is no road to it. No wheeled thing has ever been seen in its streets. The crest of the Pyrenees (which are here both precipitous and extremely high) is not a ridge nor an edge, but a great wall of slabs, as it were, leaning up against the sky. Through a crack in this wall, between two of these huge slabs, the mountaineers for many thousand years have wormed their way across the hills, but the height and the extreme steepness of the last four thousand feet have kept that passage isolated and ill-known. Upon the French side the path has recently been renewed; within a few yards upon the southern slope it dwindles and almost disappears.

As one so passes from the one country to the other, it is for all the world like the shutting of a door between oneself and the world. For some reason or other the impression of a civilization active to the point of distress, follows one all up the pass from the French railway to the summit of the range ; but when that summit is passed the new and brilliant sun upon the enormous glaciers before one, the absence of human signs and of water, impress one suddenly with silence.

From that point one scrambles down and down for hours into a deserted valley—all noon and afternoon and evening : on the first flats a rude path at last appears. A river begins to flow ; great waterfalls pour across one's way, and for miles upon miles one limps along and down the valley across sharp boulders such as mules go best on, and often along the bed of a stream, until at night-fall—if one has started early and has put energy into one's going, and if it is a long summer day— then at nightfall one first sees cultivated fields— patches of oats not half an acre large hanging upon the sides of the ravine wherever a little shelf of soil has formed.

So went the Two Men upon an August evening, till they came in the half-light upon something which might have been rocks or might have been ruins—grey lumps against the moon : they were the houses of a little town. A sort of gulf, winding

like a river gorge, and narrower than a column of
men, was the street that brought us in.   But just
as we feared that we should have to grope our way
to find companionship we saw that great surprise
of modern mountain villages (but not of our own
in England)—a little row of electric lamps hanging from walls of an incalculable age.

Here, in this heap of mountain stones, and led
by this last of inventions, we heard at last the
sound of music, and knew that we were near an
inn.   The Moors called (and call) an inn Fundouk ;
the Spaniards call it a Fonda.   To this Fonda,
therefore, we went, and as we went the sound of
music grew louder, till we came to a door of oak
studded with gigantic nails and swung upon
hinges which, by their careful workmanship and
the nature of their grotesques, were certainly of
the Renaissance.   Indeed, the whole of this
strange hive of mountain men was a mixture—
ignorance, sharp modernity, utter reclusion : barbaric, Christian ; ruinous and enduring things.
The more recent houses had for the most part their
dates marked above their doors.   There were some
of the sixteenth century, and many of the seventeenth, but the rest were far older, and bore no
marks at all.   There was but one house of our own
time, and as for the church, it was fortified with
narrow windows made for arrows.

Not only did the Moors call an inn a Fundouk,

but also they lived (and live) not on the ground floor, but on the first floor of their houses : so after them the Spaniards.   We came in from the street through those great oaken doors, not into a room, but into a sort of barn, with a floor of beaten earth ; from this a stair (every banister of which was separately carved in a dark wood) led up to the storey upon which the inn was held.   There was no hour for the meal.   Some were beginning to eat, some had ended.   When we asked for food it was prepared, but an hour was taken to prepare it, and it was very vile ; the wine also was a wine that tasted as much of leather as of grapes, and reminded a man more of an old saddle than of vineyards.

The people who put this before us had in their faces courage, complete innocence, carelessness, and sleep.   They spoke to us in their language (I understood it very ill) of far countries, which they did not clearly know—they hardly knew the French beyond the hills.   As no road led into their ageless village, so did no road lead out of it. To reach the great cities in the plain, and the railway eighty miles away, why, there was the telephone.   They slept at such late hours as they chose ; by midnight many were still clattering through the lane below.   No order and no law compelled them in anything.

The Two Men were asleep after this first astonishing glimpse of forgotten men and of a strange country. In the stifling air outside there was a clattering of the hoofs of mules and an argument of drivers. A long way off a man was playing a little stringed instrument, and there was also in the air a noise of insects buzzing in the night heat. When all of a sudden the whole place awoke to the noise of a piercing cry which but for its exquisite tone might have been the cry of pain, so shrill was it and so coercing to the ear. It was maintained, and before it fell was followed by a succession of those quarter-tones which only the Arabs have, and which I had thought finally banished from Europe. To this inhuman and appalling song were set loud open vowels rather than words.

Of the Two Men, one leapt at once from his bed crying out, "This is the music! This is what I have desired to hear!" For this is what he had once been told could be heard in the desert, when first he looked out over the sand from Atlas : but though he had travelled far, he had never heard it, and now he heard it here, in the very root of these European hills. It was on this account that he cried out, "This is the music!" And when he had said this he put on a great rough cloak and ran to the room from which the song or cry proceeded, and after him ran his companion.

The Two Men stood at the door behind a great

mass of muleteers, who all craned forward to where, upon a dais at the end of the room, sat a Jewess who still continued for some five minutes this intense and terrible effort of the voice. Beside her a man who was not of her race urged her on as one urges an animal to further effort, crying out, "Hap ! Hap !" and beating his palms together rhythmically and driving and goading her to the full limit of her power.

The sound ceased suddenly as though it had been stabbed and killed, and the woman whose eyes had been strained and lifted throughout as in a trance, and whose body had been rigid and quivering, sank down upon herself and let her eyelids fall, and her head bent forward.

There was complete silence from that moment till the dawn, and the second of the Two Men said to the first that they had had an experience not so much of music as of fire.

DELFT

DELFT is the most charming town in the world. It is one of the neat cities : trim, small, packed, self-contained. A good woman in early middle age, careful of her dress, combed, orderly, not without a sober beauty—such a woman on her way to church of a Sunday morning is not more pleasing than Delft. It is on the verge of monotony, yet still individual ; in one style, yet suggesting many centuries of activity. There is a full harmony of many colours, yet the memory the place leaves is of a united, warm and generous tone. Were you suddenly put down in Delft you would know very well that the vast and luxuriant meadows of Holland surrounded it, so much are its air, houses, and habits those of men inspired by the fields.

Delft is very quiet, as befits a town so many of whose streets are ordered lanes of water, yet one is inspired all the while by the voices of children, and the place is strongly alive. Over its sky there follow in stately order the great white clouds of summer, and at evening the haze is lit just barely from below with that transforming level light which is the joy and inspiration of the Netherlands.   Against such an expanse stands up for ever one of the gigantic but delicate belfries, round which these towns are gathered   For Holland, it seems, is not a country of villages, but of compact, clean towns, standing scattered over a great waste of grass like the sea.

This belfry of Delft is a thing by itself in Europe, and all these truths can be said of it by a man who sees it for the first time: first, that its enormous height is drawn up, as it were, and enhanced by every chance stroke that the instinct of its slow builders lit upon; for these men of the infinite flats love the contrast of such pinnacles, and they have made in the labour of about a thousand years a landscape of their own by building, just as they have made by ceaseless labour a rich pasture and home out of those solitary marshes of the delta.

Secondly, that height is enhanced by something which you will not see, save in the low countries between the hills of Ardennes and the yellow seas —I mean brick Gothic; for the Gothic which you and I know is built up of stone, and, even so, produces every effect of depth and distance; but the Gothic of the Netherlands is often built curiously of bricks, and the bricks are so thin that it needs a whole host of them in an infinity

of fine lines to cover a hundred feet of wall. They
fill the blank spaces with their repeated detail;
they make the style (which even in stone is full
of chances and particular corners) most intricate,
and—if one may use so exaggerated a metaphor—
"populous." Above all, they lead the eye up
and up, making a comparison and measure of
their tiny bands until the domination of a buttress
or a tower is exaggerated to the enormous. Now
the belfry of Delft, though all the upper part is of
stone, yet stands on a great pedestal (as it were)
of brick—a pedestal higher than the houses. And
in this base are pierced two towering, broad and
single ogives, empty and wonderful and full
of that untragic sadness which you may find
also in the drooping and wide eyes of extreme
old age.

Thirdly, the very structure of the thing is bells.
Here the bells are more than the soul of a Christian spire; they are its body too, its whole self.
An army of them fills up all the space between the
delicate supports and framework of the upper
parts; for I know not how many feet, in order,
diminishing in actual size and in the perspective
also of that triumphant elevation, stand ranks on
ranks of bells from the solemn to the wild, from
the large to the small; a hundred or two hundred
or a thousand. There is here the prodigality
of Brabant and Hainaut and the Batavian blood,

a generosity and a productivity in bells without stint, the man who designed it saying : "Since we are to have bells, let us have bells : not measured out, calculated, expensive, and prudent bells, but careless bells, self-answering multitudinous bells; bells without fear, bells excessive and bells innumerable ; bells worthy of the ecstasies that are best thrown out and published in the clashing of bells. For bells are single, like real pleasures, and we will combine such a great number that they shall be like the happy and complex life of a man. In a word, let us be noble and scatter our bells and reap a harvest till our town is famous for its bells." So now all the spire is more than clothed with them ; they are more than stuff or ornament ; they are an outer and yet sensitive armour, all of bells.

Nor is the wealth of these bells in their number only, but also in their use ; for they are not reserved in any way, but ring tunes and add harmonies at every half and quarter and at all the hours both by night and by day. Nor must you imagine that there is any obsession of noise through this ; they are far too high and melodious, and, what is more, too thoroughly a part of all the spirit of Delft to be more than a perpetual and half-forgotten impression of continual music ; they render its air sacred and fill it with something so akin to an uplifted silence as to leave one—when one has passed from their influence—asking what balm that was which soothed all the harshness of sound about one.

Round that tower and that voice the town hangs industrious and subdued—a family. Its waters, its intimate canals, its boats for travel, and its slight plashing of bows in the place of wheels, entered the spirit of the traveller and gave him for one long day the Right of Burgess. In autumn, in the early afternoon—the very season for those walls—it was easy for him to be filled with a restrained but united chorus, the under-voices of the city, droning and murmuring perpetually of Peace and of Labour and of the wild rose—Content. . . .

Peace, labour, and content—three very good words, and summing up, perhaps, the goal of all mankind. Of course, there is a problem everywhere, and it would be heresy to say that the people of Delft have solved it. It is Matter of Breviary that the progress of our lives is but asymptotic to true joy; we can approach it nearer and nearer, but we can never reach it.

Nevertheless, I say that in this excellent city, though it is outside Eden, you may, when the wind is in the right quarter, receive in distant and rare appeals the scent and air of Paradise; the soul is filled.

To this emotion there corresponds and shall here

be quoted a very noble verse, which runs—or
rather glides—as follows :—

> Satiety, that momentary flower
> Stretched to an hour—
> These are her gifts which all mankind may use,
> And all refuse.

Or words to that effect.   And to think that you
can get to a place like that for less than a pound !

THE WING OF DALUA

TIME was, and that not so long ago, when the Two Men had revealed to them by their Genius a corner of Europe wherein they were promised more surprises and delights than in any other.

It was secretly made known to them that in this place there were no pictures, and that no one had praised its people, and further that no Saint had ever troubled it; and the rich and all their evils (so the two men were assured) had never known the place at all.

It was under the influence of such a message that they at once began walking at great speed for the river which is called the River of Gold, and for the valleys of Andorra; and since it seemed that other men had dared to cross the Pyrenees and to see the Republic, and since it seemed also, according to books, records and what not, that may have been truth or may have been lies, that common men so doing went always by one way, called the Way of Hospitalet, the Two Men determined to go by no such common path, but to march, all clothed with power, in a straight line, and to take the main range of the mountains just where they chose, and to come down upon the Andorrans unexpectedly and to deserve their admiration and perhaps their fear.

They chose, therefore, upon the map the valley of that torrent called the Aston, and before it was evening, but at an hour when the light of the sun was already very ripe and low they stood under a great rock called Guie, which was all of bare limestone with façades as bare as the Yosemite, and almost as clean.   They looked up at this great rock of Guie and made it the terminal of their attempt.   I was one and my companion was the other : these were the two men who started out before a sunset in August to conquer the high Pyrenees. Before me was a very deep valley full of woods, and reaching higher and higher perpetually so that it reminded me of Hyperion; but as for my companion, it reminded him of nothing, for he said loudly that he had never seen any such things before and had never believed that summits of so astonishing a height were to be found on earth. Not even at night had he imagined such appalling upward and upward into the sky, and this he said though he had seen the Alps, of which it is true that when you are close to them they are very middling affairs ; but not so the Pyrenees, which are not only great but also terrible, for they are haunted, as you shall hear. But before I begin to write of the spirits that inhabit the deserts of the Aston, I must first explain, for the sake of those who have not seen them, how the awful valleys of the Pyrenees are made.

All the high valleys of mountains go in steps, but those of the Pyrenees in a manner more regular even than those of the Sierra Nevada out in California, which the Pyrenees so greatly resemble. For the steps here are nearly always three in number between the plain and the main chain, and each is entered by a regular gate of rock. So it is in the valley of the Ariege, and so it is in that of the Aston, and so it is in every other valley until you get to the far end where live the cleanly but incomprehensible Basques. Each of these steps is perfectly level, somewhat oval in shape, a mile or two or sometimes five miles long, but not often a mile broad. Through each will run the river of the valley, and upon either side of it there will be rich pastures, and a high plain of this sort is called a *jasse*, the same as in California is called a " flat " : as " Dutch Flat," " Poverty Flat," and other famous flats.

First then will come a great gorge through which one marches up from the plain, and then at the head of it very often a waterfall of some kind, along the side of which one forces one's way up painfully through a narrow chasm of rock and finds

above one the great green level of the first jasse
with the mountains standing solemnly around it.
And then when one has marched all along this
level one will come to another gorge and another
chasm, and when one has climbed over the barrier
of rock and risen up another 2000 feet or so, one
comes to a second jasse, smaller as a rule than the
lower one ; but so high are the mountains that all
this climbing into the heart of them does not seem
to have reduced their height at all.   And then
one marches along this second jasse and one comes
to yet another gorge and climbs up just as one did
the two others, through a chasm where there will
be a little waterfall or a large one, and one finds at
the top the smallest and most lonely of the jasses.
This often has a lake in it.   The mountains round
it will usually be cliffs, forming sometimes a perfect
ring, and so called cirques, or, by the Spaniards,
cooking-pots ; and as one stands on the level floor
of one such last highest jasse and looks up at the
summit of the cliffs, one knows that one is looking
at the ridge of the main chain.   Then it is one's
business, if one desires to conquer the high
Pyrenees, to find a sloping place up the cliffs to
reach their summits and to go down into the
further Spanish valleys.   This is the order of the
Pyrenean dale, and this was the order of that of
the Aston.

Up the gorge then we went, my companion and

I ; the day fell as we marched, and there was a
great moon out, filling the still air, when we came
to the first chasm, and climbing through it saw
before us, spread with a light mist over its pastures,
the first jasse under the moonlight. And up we
went, and up again, to the end of the second jasse,
having before us the vast wall of the main range,
and in our hearts a fear that there was something
unblessed in the sight of it. For though neither I
told it to my companion nor he to me, we had both
begun to feel a fear which the shepherds of these
mountains know very well. It was perhaps midnight or a little more when we made our camp,
after looking in vain for a hut which may once
have stood there, but now stood no longer. We
lit a fire, but did not overcome the cold, which
tormented us throughout the night, for the wind
blew off the summits ; and at last we woke from
our half-sleep and spent the miserable hours in
watching the Great Bear creeping round the pole,
and in trying to feed the dying embers with damp
fuel. And there it was that I discovered what I
now make known to the world, namely, that gorse
and holly will burn of themselves, even while they
are yet rooted in the ground. So we sat sleepless
and exhausted, and not without misgiving, for we
had meant that night before camping to be right
under the foot of the last cliffs, and we were yet
many miles away. We were glad to see the river

at last in the meadows show plainly under the growing light, the rocks turning red upon the sky-line, and the extinction of the stars.   As we so looked north and eastward the great rock of Guie stood up all its thousands of feet enormous against the rising of the sun.

We were very weary, and invigorated by nothing but the light, but, having that at least to strengthen us, we made at once for the main range, knowing very well that, once we were over it, it would be downhill all the way, and seeing upon our maps that there were houses and living men high in the further Andorran valley, which was not deserted like this vale of the Aston, but inhabited : full, that is, of Catalans, who would soon make us forget the inhuman loneliness of the heights, for by this time we were both convinced, though still neither of us said it to the other, that there was an evil brooding over all this place.

It was noon when, after many hours of broken marching and stumbling, which betrayed our weak-ness, we stood at last beside the tarn in which the last cliffs of the ridge are reflected, and here was a steep slope up which a man could scramble.   We drank at the foot of it the last of our wine and ate the last of our bread, promising ourselves refresh-ment, light, and peace immediately upon the further side, and thus lightened of our provisions, and with more heart in us, we assaulted the final

hill ; but just at the summit, where there should
have greeted us a great view over Spain, there
lowered upon us the angry folds of a black cloud,
and the first of the accidents that were set in order
by some enemy to ruin us fell upon my companion
and me.

For a storm broke, and that with such violence
that we thought it would have shattered the bare
hills, for an infernal thunder crashed from one
precipice to another, and there flashed, now close
to us, now vividly but far off, in the thickness of
the cloud, great useless and blinding glares of
lightning, and hailstones of great size fell about
us also, leaping from the bare rocks like marbles.
And when the rain fell it was just as though it had
been from a hose, forced at one by a pressure
instead of falling, and we two on that height were
the sole objects of so much fury, until at last my
companion cried out from the rock beneath which
he was cowering, "This is intolerable !"   And I
answered him, from the rock which barely covered
me, "It is not to be borne !"   So in the midst of
the storm we groped our way down into the valley
beneath, and got below the cloud ; and when we
were there we thought we had saved the day, for
surely we were upon the southern side of the hills,
and in a very little while we should see the first
roofs of the Andorrans.

For two doubtful hours we trudged down that

higher valley, but there were no men, nor any trace of men except this, that here and there the semblance of a path appeared, especially where the valley fell rapidly from one stage to another over smooth rocks, which, in their least dangerous descent, showed by smooth scratches the passage of some lost animal. For the rest, nothing human nor the memory of it was there to comfort us, though in one place we found a group of cattle browsing alone without a master. There we sat down in our exhaustion and confessed at last what every hour had inwardly convinced us of with greater strength, that we were not our own masters, that there was trouble and fate all round us, that we did not know what valley this might be, and that the storm had been but the beginning of an unholy adventure. We had been snared into Fairyland.

We did not speak much together, for fear of lowering our hearts yet more by the confession one to the other of the things we knew to be true. We did not tell each other what reserve of courage remained to us, or of strength. We sat and looked at the peaks immeasurably above us, and at the veils of rain between them, and at the black background of the sky. Nor was there anything in the landscape which did not seem to us unearthly and forlorn.

It was, in a manner, more lonely than had been

the very silence of the further slope: there was less to comfort and support the soul of a man; but with every step downward we were penetrated more and more with the presence of things not mortal and of influences to which any desolation was preferable. At one moment voices called to us from the water, at another we heard our names, but pronounced in a whisper so slight and so exact that the more certain we were of hearing them the less did we dare to admit the reality of what we had heard. In a third place we saw twice in succession, though we were still going forward, the same tree standing by the same stone: for neither tree nor stone was natural to the good world, but each had been put there by whatever was mocking us and drawing us on.

Already had we stumbled twice and thrice the distance that should have separated us from the first Andorran village, but we had seen nothing, not a wall, nor smoke from a fire, let alone the tower of a Christian church, or the houses of men. Nor did any length of the way now make us wonder more than we had already wondered, nor did we hope, however far we might proceed, that we should be saved unless some other influence could be found to save us from the unseen masters of this place. For by this time we had need of mutual comfort, and openly said it to one another—but in low tones—that the valley was Faëry. The river went on calling to us all the while. In places it was full of distant cheering, in others crowded with the laughter of a present multitude of tiny things, and always mocking us with innumerable tenuous voices. It grew to be evening. It was nearly two days since we had seen a man.

There stood in the broader and lower part of the valley to which we had now come, numerous rocks and boulders; for our deception some one of them or another would seem to be a man. I heard my companion call suddenly, as though to a stranger, and as he called I thought that he had indeed perceived the face of a human being, and I felt a sort of sudden health in me when I heard the tone of his voice; and when I looked up I also saw a man. We came towards him and he did not move. Close up beside his form we put out our hands: but what we touched was a rough and silent stone.

After that we spoke no more. We went on through the gathering twilight, determined to march downwards to the end, but knowing pretty well what the end would be. Once only did we again fall into the traps that were laid about us, when we went and knocked at the hillside where we thought we had seen a cottage and its oaken door, and after the mockery of that disappointment we would not be deceived again, nor make our-

selves again the victims of the laughter that perpetually proceeded from the torrent.

The path led us onwards in a manner that was
all one with the plot now woven round our feet.
We could but follow the path, though we knew with
what an evil purpose it was made: that it was as
phantom as the rest.   At one place it invited us to
cross, upon two shaking pine trunks, the abyss of a
cataract ; in another it invited us to climb, in spite
of our final weariness, a great barrier of rock that
lay between an upper and a lower jasse.   We
continued upon it determinedly, with heads bent,
barely hoping that perhaps at last we should emerge
from this haunted ground, but the illusions which
had first mocked us we resolutely refused.   So much
so, that where at one place there stood plainly before
us in the gathering darkness a farm-house with its
trees and its close, its orchard and its garden gate,
I said to my companion, " All this place is cursed,
and I will not go near."   And he applauded me,
for he knew as well as I that if we had gone a few
steps towards that orchard and that garden close,
they would have turned into the bracken of the hillside, bare granite and unfruitful scree.

The main range, where it appeared in revelations behind us through the clouds, was far higher
than mountains ever seem to waking men, and
it stood quite sheer as might a precipice in a
dream.   The forests upon either side ran up until

they were lost miles and miles above us in the storm.

Night fell and we still went onward, the one never daring to fall far behind the other, and once or twice in an hour calling to each other to make sure that another man was near; but this we did not continue, because as we went on each of us became aware under the midnight of the presence of a Third.

.   .   .   .   .   .

There was a place where the path, now broad and plain, approached a sort of little sandy bay going down towards the stream, and there I saw, by a sudden glimpse of the moon through the clouds, a large cave standing wide. We went down to it in silence, we gathered brushwood, we lit a fire, and we lay down in the cave. But before we lay down I said to my companion : " I have seen the moon—she is in the *north*. Into what place have we come?" He said to me in answer : " Nothing here is earthly," and after he had said this we both fell into a profound sleep in which we forgot not only cold, great hunger and fatigue, but our own names and our very souls, and passed, as it were, into a deep bath of forgetfulness.

When we woke at the same moment, it was dawn.

We stood up in the clear and happy light and found that everything was changed. We poured water upon our faces and our hands, strode out a hundred yards and saw again the features of a man. He had a kind face of some age, and eyes such as are the eyes of mountaineers, which seem to have constantly contemplated distant horizons and wide plains beneath their homes. We heard as he came up the sound of a bell in a Christian church below, and we exchanged with him the salutations of living men. Then I said to him : " What day is this ? " He said " Sunday," and a sort of memory of our fear came on us, for we had lost a day.

Then I said to him : " What river are we upon, and what valley is this ? "

He answered : " The river and the valley of the Aston." And what he said was true, for as we rounded a corner we perceived right before us a barrier, that rock of Guie from which we had set out. We had come down again into France, and into the very dale by which we had begun our ascent.

But what that valley was which had led us from the summits round backward to our starting-place, forcing upon us the refusal of whatever powers protect this passage of the chain, I have never been able to tell. It is not upon the maps ; by our description the peasants knew nothing of it. No book tells of it. No men except ourselves have seen it, and I am willing to believe that it is not of this world.

ON ELY

THERE are two ways by which a man may acquire any kind of learning or profit, and this is especially true of travel.

Everybody knows that one can increase what one has of knowledge or of any other possession by going outwards and outwards; but what is also true, and what people know less, is that one can increase it by going inwards and inwards. There is no goal to either of these directions, nor any term to your advantage as you travel in them.

If you will be extensive, take it easy; the infinite is always well ahead of you, and its symbol is the sky.

If you will be intensive, hurry as much as you like you will never exhaust the complexity of things; and the truth of this is very evident in a garden, or even more in the nature of insects; of which beasts I have heard it said that the most stolid man in the longest of lives would acquire only a cursory knowledge of even one kind, as, for instance, of the horned beetle, which sings so angrily at evening.

You may travel for the sake of great horizons, and travel all your life, and fill your memory with nothing but views from mountain-tops, and yet not have seen a tenth of the world. Or you may spend !your life upon the religious history of East Rutland, and plan the most enormous book upon it, and yet find that you have continually to excise and select from the growing mass of your material.

.   .   .   .   .   .

A wise man having told me this some days before (and I having believed it), it seemed to me as though a new entertainment had been invented for me, or rather as though I had found a bottomless purse ; since by this doctrine there was manifestly no end to the number of my pleasures, and to each of this infinite number no possibility of exhaustion ; but I thought I would put it to the test in this way : putting aside but three days, I determined in that space to explore a little corner of this country.

Now, although I saw not one-hundredth of the buildings or the people in this very small space, and though I knew nothing of the birds or the beasts or the method of tillage, or of anything of all that makes up a land, yet I saw enough to fill a book. And the pleasure of my thoughts was so great that I determined to pick out a bit here and a bit there, and to put down the notes almost without arrangement, in order that those who cannot do these things (whether from lack of leisure or for some other reason) may get some part of my pleasure without loss to me (on the contrary, with profit); and in order that every one may be convinced of what this little journey finally taught me, and which I repeat—that there is an inexhaustible treasure everywhere, not only outwards, but inwards.

I had known the Ouse—(how many years ago!) —I had looked up at those towers of Ely from my boat ; but a town from a river and a town from the street are two different things. Moreover, in that time I speak of, the day years ago, it was blowing very hard from the south, and I was anxious to be away before it, and away I went down to Lynn at one stretch ; for in those days the wind and the water seemed of more moment than old stones. Now (after how many years!) it was my business to go up by land, and as I went, the weight of the Cathedral filled the sky before me.

Impressions of this sort are explained by every man in his own way—for my part I felt the Norman.

I know not by what accident it was, but never had I come so nearly into the presence of the men who founded England. The isolation of the hill, the absence of clamour and false noise and everything modern, the smallness of the village, the solidity and amplitude of the homes and their security, all recalled an origin.

I went into the door of the Cathedral under the high tower. I noted the ponderous simplicity of the great squat pillars, the rough capitals—plain bulges of stone without so much as a pattern cut upon them—the round arch and the low aisles; but in one corner remaining near the door—a baptistery, I suppose—was a crowd of ornament which (like everything of that age) bore the mark of simplicity, for it was an endless heap of the arch and the column and the zigzag ornament— the broken line. Its richness was due to nothing but the repetition of similar forms, and everywhere the low stature, the muscles, the broad shoulders of the thing, proved and reawoke the memory of the Norman soldiers.

They have been written of enough to-day, but who has seen them from close by or understood that brilliant interlude of power?

The little bullet-headed men, vivacious, and splendidly brave, we know that they awoke all Europe, that they first provided settled financial systems and settled governments of land, and that everywhere, from the Grampians to Mesopotamia, they were like steel when all other Christians were like wood or like lead.

We know that they were a flash. They were not formed or definable at all before the year 1000; by the year 1200 they were gone. Some odd transitory phenomenon of cross-breeding, a very lucky freak in the history of the European family, produced the only body of men who all were lords and who in their collective action showed continually nothing but genius.

We know that they were the spear-head, as it were, of the Gallic spirit : the vanguard of that one of the Gallic expansions which we associate with the opening of the Middle Ages and with the Crusades. . . . We know all this and write about it ; nevertheless, we do not make enough of the Normans in England.

Here and there a man who really knows his subject and who disdains the market of the school books, puts as it should be put their conquest of this island and their bringing into our blood whatever is still strongest in it.   Many (descended from their leaders) have remarked their magical ride through South Italy, their ordering of Sicily, their hand in Palestine.   As for the Normans in Normandy, of their exchequer there, of what Rouen was—all that has never been properly written down at all.   Their great adventure here in England has been most written of by far; but I say again no one has made enough of them ; no one has brought them back out of their graves. The character of what they did has been lost in these silly little modern quarrels about races, which are but the unscholarly expression of a deeper hypocritical quarrel about religion.

Yet it is in England that the Norman can be studied as he can be studied nowhere else. He did not write here (as in Sicily) upon a palimpsest. He was not merged here (as in the Orient) with the rest of the French. He was segregated here ; he can be studied in isolation ; for though so many that crossed the sea on that September night with William, the big leader of them, held no Norman tenure, yet the spirit of the whole thing was Norman : the regularity, the suddenness, the achievement, and, when the short fighting was over, the creation of a new society. It was the Norman who began everything over again—the first fresh influence since Rome.

The riot of building has not been seized. The island was conquered in 1070. It was a place of heavy foolish men with random laws, pale eyes, and a slow manner ; their houses were of wood : sometimes they built (but how painfully, and how childishly !) with stone. There was no height, there was no dignity, there was no sense of permanence. The Norman Government was established. At once rapidity, energy, the clear object of a united and organized power followed. And see what followed in architecture alone, and in what a little space of the earth, and in what a little stretch of time—less than the time that separates us to-day from the year of Disraeli's death or the occupation of Egypt.

The Conquest was achieved in 1070. In that same year they pulled down the wooden shed at Bury St. Edmunds, "unworthy," they said, "of a great saint," and began the great shrine of stone. Next year it was the castle at Oxford, in 1075 Monkswearmouth, Jarrow, and the church at Chester; in 1077 Rochester and St. Albans; in 1079 Winchester. Ely, Worcester, Thorney, Hurley, Lincoln followed with the next years; by 1089 they had tackled Gloucester, by 1092 Carlisle, by 1093 Lindisfarne, Christchurch—tall Durham. . . . And this is but a short and random list of some of their greatest works in the space of one boyhood. Hundreds of castles, houses, village churches are unrecorded.

Were they not indeed a people? . . . And all that effort realized itself before Pope Urban had made the speech which launched the armies against the Holy Land. The Norman had created and founded all this before the Mass of Europe was urged against the flame of the Arab, to grow fruitful and to be transformed.

One may say of the Norman preceding the Gothic what Dante said of Virgil preceding the Faith: Would that they had been born in a time when they could have known it! But the East was not yet open. The mind of Europe had not yet received the great experience of the Crusades; the Normans had no medium wherein to express their mighty soul, save the round arch and the straight line, the capital barbaric or naked, the sullen round shaft of the pillar—more like a drum than like a column. They could build, as it were, with nothing but the last ruins of Rome. They were given no forms but the forms which the fatigue and lethargy of the Dark Ages had repeated for six hundred years. They were capable, even in the north, of impressing even these forms with a superhuman majesty.

.   .   .   .   .   .

Was I not right in saying that everywhere in the world one can look in and in and never find an end to one's delight? I began to explore but a tiny corner of England, and here in one corner of that corner and in but one thought arising from this corner of a corner I have found these things.

.   .   .   .   .   .

But England is especially a garden of this sort, or a storehouse; and in nothing more than in this matter of the old architecture which perpetuates the barbaric grandeur of the eleventh century—the time before it was full day.

When the Gothic came the whole of northern Europe was so enamoured of it that common men, bishops, and kings pulled down and rebuilt everywhere. Old crumbling walls of the Romanesque

fell at Amiens ; you can still see them cowering at
Beauvais; only an accident of fire destroyed them in
Notre Dame.   In England the transition survived;
nowhere save in England is the northern Romanesque triumphant, not even at Caen.   Elsewhere
the Gothic has conquered.   Only here in England
can you see the Romanesque facing, like an equal,
newer things, because here only was there a great
outburst of building—a kind of false spring before
the Gothic came, because here only in Europe had
a great political change and a great flood of wealth
come in before the expansion of the twelfth century
began.

There, is one little corner of England ; here is
another.

The Isle of Ely lying on the fens is like a star-
fish lying on a flat shore at low tide.   Southward,
westward, and northward from the head or centre
of the clump (which is where the Cathedral stands)
it throws out arms every way, and these arms have
each short tentacles of their own.   In between the
spurs runs the even fen like a calm sea, and on the
crest of the spurs, radiating also from Ely, run
the roads.   Long ago there was but one road of
these that linked up the Isle with the rest of
England.   It was the road from the south, and
there the Romans had a station ; the others led
only to the farms and villages dependent upon the

city. Now they are prolonged by artifice into the modern causeways which run over the lower and new-made land.

The Isle has always stood like a fortress, and has always had a title and a commandership, which once were very real things ; the people told me that the King of England's third title was Marquis of Ely, and I knew of myself that just before the civil wars the commandership of the Isle gave the power of raising men.

The ends of many wars drifted to this place to die. Here was the last turn of the Saxon lords, and the last rally of the feudal rebellions of the thirteenth century.

Not that the fens were impassable or homeless, but they were difficult in patches ; their paths were rare and laid upon no general system. Their inhabited fields were isolated, their waters tidal, with great banks of treacherous mud, intricate and unbridged ; such conditions are amply suffi- cient for a defensive war. The flight of a small body in such a land can always baffle an army until that small body is thrust into some one refuge so well defended by marsh or river that the very defence cuts off retreat : and a small body so brought to bay in such a place has this further advantage, that from the bits of higher land, the "Islands," one of the first requirements of defence is afforded—an unbroken view of every avenue by which attack can come.   There is no surprising such forts.

.   .   .   .   .   .

So much is in Ely to-day and a great deal more. For instance (a third and last idea out of the thousand that Ely arouses), Ely is dumb and yet oracular.   The town and the hill tell you nothing till you have studied them in silence and for some considerable time.   This boast is made by many towns, that they hold a secret.   But Ely, which is rather a village than a town, has alone a true claim.   The proof of which is this, that no one comes to Ely for a few hours and carries anything away, whereas no man lives in Ely for a year without beginning to write a book.   I do not say that all are published, but I swear that all are begun.

THE INN OF THE MARGERIDE

WHATEVER, keeping its proportion and form, is designed upon a scale much greater or much less than that of our general experience, produces upon the mind an effect of phantasy.

A little perfect model of an engine or a ship does not only amuse or surprise. It rather casts over the imagination something of that veil through which the world is transfigured, and which I have called "the wing of Dalua"; the medium of appreciations beyond experience; the medium of vision, of original passion and of dreams. The principal spell of childhood returns as we bend over the astonishing details. We are giants—or there is no secure standard left in our intelligence.

So it is with the common thing built much larger than the million examples upon which we had based our petty security. It has been always in the nature of worship that heroes, or the gods made manifest, should be men, but larger than men. Not tall men or men grander, but men transcendent: men only in their form; in their dimension so much superior as to be lifted out

55

of our world.   An arch as old as Rome but not
yet ruined, found on the sands of Africa, arrests
the traveller in this fashion.   In his modern cities
he has seen greater things ; but here in Africa,
where men build so squat and punily, cowering
under the heat upon the parched ground, so noble
and so considerable a span, carved as men can
carve under sober and temperate skies, catches the
mind, and clothes it with a sense of the strange.
And of these emotions the strongest, perhaps, is
that which most of those who travel to-day go
seeking ; the enchantment of mountains : the air
by which we know them for something utterly
different from high hills.   Accustomed to the contour of downs and tors, or to the valleys and long
slopes that introduce a range, we come to some
wider horizon and see, far off, a further line of
hills.   To hills all the mind is attuned : a moderate
ecstasy.   The clouds are above the hills, lying
level in the empty sky ; men and their ploughs
have visited, it seems, all the land about us.   Till,
suddenly, faint but hard, a cloud less varied, a
greyer portion of the infinite sky itself, is seen to
be permanent above the world.   Then all our
grasp of the wide view breaks down.   We change.
The valleys and the tiny towns, the unseen mites
of men, the gleams or threads of roads, are pros-
trate, covering a little watching space before the
shrine of this dominant and towering presence.

It is as though humanity were permitted to break through the vulgar illusion of daily sense, and to learn in a physical experience how unreal are all the absolute standards by which we build. It is as though the vast and the unexpected had a purpose, and that purpose were the showing to mankind in rare glimpses what places are designed for the soul—those ultimate places where things common become shadows and fail, and the divine part in us, which adores and desires, breathes its own air, and is at last alive.

.   .   .   .   .   .

This awful charm which attaches to the enormous envelops the Causse of Mende; for its attributes are all of them pushed beyond the ordinary limit.

Each of the four Causses is a waste; but the Causse of Mende is utterly bereft of men. Each is a high plateau; but this, I believe, the highest in feet, and certainly in impression. You stand there as it were upon the summit of a lonely pedestal, with nothing but a rocky edge around you. Each is dried up; but the Causse of Mende is without so much as a dew-pan or a well; it is wrinkled, horny, and cauterized under the alternate frost and flame of its fierce open sky, as are the deserts of the moon. Each of the Causses is silent; but the silence of the Causse of Mende is scorched and frozen into its stones, and is as old as they: all around, the torrents which have sawn their black cañons upon every side of the block frame this silence with their rumble. Each of the Causses casts up above its plain fantastic heaps of rock consonant to the wild spirit of its isolation ; but the Causse of Mende holds a kind of fortress— a medley so like the ghost of a dead town that, even in full daylight, you expect the footsteps of men ; and by night, as you go gently, in fear of waking the sleepers, you tread quite certainly among built houses and spires. This place the peasants of the cañons have called "The Old City"; and no one living will go near it who knows it well.

The Causses have also this peculiar to them : that the ravines by which each is cut off are steep and sudden. But the cliffs of the Causse of Mende are walls. That the chief of these walls may seem the more terrible, it is turned northward, so that by day and night it is in shadow, and falls sheer.

.   .   .   .   .   .

It was when I had abandoned this desolate wonder (but with its influence strong upon me) that I left the town of Mende, down on the noise of its river, and began to climb the opposing mountain of the Margeride.

It was already evening, though as yet there were no stars. The air was fresh, because the year was at that season when it is summer in the vineyard plains, but winter in the hills. A twilight so coloured and translucent as to suggest cold spanned like an Aurora the western mouth of the gully. Upon my eastward and upward way the full moon, not yet risen, began to throw an uncertain glory over the sky.

This road was made by the French Kings when their influence had crept so far south as to control these mountains. They became despots, and their despotism, which was everywhere magnificent, engraved itself upon these untenanted bare rocks. They strengthened and fortified the road. Its grandeur in so empty and impoverished a land was a boast or a threat of their power. The Republic succeeded the kings, the Armies succeeded the Republic, and every experiment succeeded the victories and the breakdown of the Armies. The road grew stronger all the while, bridging this desert, and giving pledge that the brain of Paris was able, and more able, to order the whole of the soil. So then, as I followed it, it seemed to me to bear in itself, and in its contrast with untamed surroundings, the history and the character of this one nation out of the many which live by the tradition of Europe. As I followed it and saw its exact gradient, its hard and even surface, its square border stones, and, every hundred yards, its carved mark of the distance done, these elaborations, standing quite new among the tumbled rocks of a vague upland, made one certain that Paris had been at work. Very far back (how far was marked on the milestone) the road had left the swarming gate of Toulouse. Very far on (how far was marked on the milestone) it was to cross the Saône by its own bridge, and feed the life of Lyons. In between it met and surmounted (still civilized, easy, and complete) this barbaric watershed of the Margeride.

As I followed it, law—good law and evil—seemed to go with me up the mountain side.

There was more sound than on the arid wastes of the Causse. There were trees, and birds in the trees, moving faintly. The great moon, which had now risen, shone also upon scanty grass and (from time to time) upon the trickle of water passing in runnels beneath the road.

The torrent in the depth below roared openly and strong, and, beyond it, the black wall of the Causse, immense and battlemented above me under the moon, made what poor life this mountain supported seem for a moment gracious by comparison. I remembered that sheep and goats and men could live on the Margeride.

But the Margeride has rightly compelled its very few historians to melancholy or fear.

It is a district, or a mountain range, or a single summit, which cuts off the east from the west, the Loire from the Gironde : a long even barrow of dark stone. Its people are one, suspicious of the plains. Its line against the sky is also one: no critical height in Europe is so strict and unbroken. You may see it from a long way east—from the Velay, or even from the last of the Forèz, and wonder whether it is land or a sullen bar of black cloud.

All the world knows how snow, even in mere gullies and streaks, uplifts a mountain. Well, I have seen the dull roof-tile of the Margeride from above Puy in spring, when patches of snow still clung to it, and the snow did no more than it would have done to a plain. It neither raised nor distinguished this brooding thing.

But it is indeed a barrier. Its rounded top is more formidable than if it were a ridge of rock; its saddle, broad and indeterminate, deceives the traveller, with new slight slopes following one upon the other when the sharp first of the ascent is done.

Already the last edge of the Causse beyond the valley had disappeared, and already had the great road taken me higher than the buttress which holds up that table-land, when, thinking I had gained the summit, I turned a corner in the way and found a vague roll of rising land before me. Upon this also, under the strong moonlight, I saw the ruin of a mill. Water, therefore, must have risen behind it. I expected and found yet another uncertain height, and beyond it a third, and, a mile beyond, another. This summit was like those random marshy steps which rise continually and wearily between the sluggish rivers of the prairies.

I passed the fields that gave his title to La Peyrouse. The cold, which with every hundred feet had increased unnoticed, now first disturbed me. The wind had risen (for I had come to that last stretch of the glacis, over which from beyond the final height, an eastern wind can blow), and this wind carried I know not what dust of ice, that did not make a perceptible fall, yet in an hour covered my clothes with tiny spangles, and stung upon the face like Highland snow in a gale. With that wind and that fine powdery frost went no apparent clouds. The sky was still clear above me. Such rare stars as can conquer the full moon shone palely; but round the moon herself bent an evanescent halo, like those one sees over the Channel upon clear nights before a stormy morning. The spindrift of fine ice had, I think, defined this halo.

How long I climbed through the night I do not know. The summit was but a slight accident upon a tumbled plain. The ponds stood thick with ice, the sound of running water had ceased, when the slight downward of the road through a barren moor and past broad undrained films of frozen bog, told me that I was on the further northern slope. The wind also was now roaring over the platform of the watershed, and great patches of whirling snow lay to the right and left like sand upon the grassy dunes of a coast.

Through all this loneliness and cold I went down, with the great road for a companion. Majesty and power were imposed by it upon these savage wilds. The hours uncalculated, and the long arrears of the night, had confused my attention ; the wind, the little arrows of the ice, the absence of ploughlands and of men. Those standards of measure which (I have said) the Causses so easily disturb would not return to me. I took mile after mile almost unheeding, numbed with cold, demanding sleep, but ignorant of where might be found the next habitation.

It was in this mood that I noted on a distant swirl of rocks before me what might have been roofs and walls ; but in that haunted country the rocks play such tricks as I have told. The moonlight also, which seems so much too bright upon a lonely heath, fails one altogether when distinction must be made between distant things, and when men are near. I did not know that these rocks (or houses) were the high group of Chateauneuf till I came suddenly upon the long and low house which stands below it on the road, and is the highway inn for the mountain town beyond.

I halted for a moment, because no light came from the windows. Just opposite the house a great tomb marked the fall of some hero. The wind seemed less violent. The waters of the marshy plain had gathered. They were no longer frozen, and a little brook ran by. As I waited there, hesitating, my fatigue came upon me, and I knocked at their great door. They opened, and light poured upon the road, and the noise of peasants talking loudly, and the roaring welcome of a fire. In this way I ended my crossing of these sombre and unrecorded hills.

·   ·   ·   ·   ·   ·

I that had lost count of hours and of heights in the glamour of the midnight and of the huge abandoned places of my climb, stepped now into a hall where the centuries also mingled and lost their order. The dancing fire filled one of those great pent-house chimneys that witness to the communal life of the Middle Ages. Around and above it, ironwork of a hundred years branched from the inglenooks to support the drying meats of the winter provision. A wide board, rude, over-massive, and shining with long usage, reflected the stone ware and the wine. Chairs, carved grotesquely, and as old almost as the walls about me, stood round the comfort of the fire. I saw that the windows were deeper than a man's arms could reach, and wedge-shaped—made for fighting. I saw that the beams of the high roof, which the fire-light hardly caught, were black oak and squared enormously, like the ribs of a master-galley, and in the leaves and garden things that hung from them, in the mighty stones of the wall, and the beaten earth of the floor, the strong simplicity of our past, and the promise of our endurance, came upon me.

The peasants sitting about the board and fire had risen, looking at the door ; for strangers were rare, and it was very late as I came out of the empty cold into that human room. Their dress was ancestral ; the master, as he spoke to me, mixed new words with old. He had phrases that the Black Prince used when he went riding at arms across the Margeride. He spoke also of modern things, of the news in the valley from which I had come, and the railway and Puy below us. They put before me bread and wine, which I most needed. I sat right up against the blaze. We all talked high together of the things we knew. For when I had told them what news there was in the valley, they also answered my questions, into which I wove as best I could those still living ancient words I had caught from their mouths. I asked them whose was that great tomb under the moonlight, at which I had shuddered as I entered their doors. They told me it was Duguesclin's tomb ; for he got his death-wound here under the walls of the town above us five hundred years ago, and in this house he had died. Then I asked what stream that was which trickled from the half-frozen moss, and led down the valley of my next day's journey. They told me it was called the River Red-cap, and they said that it was Faëry. I asked them also what was the name of the height over which I had come; they answered, that the shepherds called it "The King's House," and that hence, in clear weather, under an eastern wind, one could see far off, beyond the Velay, that lonely height which is called "The Chair of God."

So we talked together, drinking wine and telling each other of many things, I of the world to which I was compelled to return, and they of the pastures and the streams, and all the story of Lozère. And, all the while, not the antiquity alone, but the endurance, of Christendom poured into me from every influence around.

They rose to go to the homes which were their own, without a lord. We exchanged the last salutations. The wooden soles of their shoes clattered upon the stone threshold of the door.

The master also rose and left me. I sat there for perhaps an hour, alone, with the falling fire before me and a vision in my heart.

Though I was here on the very roof and centre of the western land, I heard the surge of the inner and the roll of the outer sea; the foam broke against the Hebrides, and made a white margin to the cliffs of Holy Ireland. The tide poured up beyond our islands to the darkness in the north. I saw the German towns, and Lombardy, and the

light on Rome. And the great landscape I saw
from the summit to which I was exalted was not
of to-day only, but also of yesterday, and perhaps
of to-morrow.

Our Europe cannot perish. Her religion—which
is also mine—has in it those victorious energies of
defence which neither merchants nor philosophers
can understand, and which are yet the prime
condition of establishment. Europe, though she
must always repel attacks from within and from
without, is always secure; the soul of her is a
certain spirit, at once reasonable and chivalric.
And the gates of Hell shall not prevail against it.

She will not dissolve by expansion, nor be
broken by internal strains. She will not suffer
that loss of unity which would be for all her
members death, and for her history and meaning
and self an utter oblivion. She will certainly
remain.

Her component peoples have merged and have
remerged. Her particular, famous cities have
fallen down. Her soldiers have believed the
world to have lost all, because a battle turned
against them, Hittin or Leipsic. Her best has at
times grown poor, and her worst rich. Her colo-
nies have seemed dangerous for a moment from
the insolence of their power, and then again (for
a moment) from the contamination of their decline. She has suffered invasion of every sort;

the East has wounded her in arms and has corrupted her with ideas; her vigorous blood has healed the wounds at once, and her permanent sanity has turned such corruptions into innocuous follies.   She will certainly remain.

.   .   .   .   .   .

So that old room, by its very age, reminded me, not of decay, but of unchangeable things.

All this came to me out of the fire; and upon such a scene passed the pageantry of our astounding history.   The armies marching perpetually, the guns and ring of bronze; I heard the chaunt of our prayers.   And, though so great a host went by from the Baltic to the passes of the Pyrenees, the myriads were contained in one figure common to them all.

I was refreshed, as though by the resurrection of something loved and thought dead.   I was no longer afraid of Time.

That night I slept ten hours.   Next day, as I swung out into the air, I knew that whatever Power comforts men had thrown wide open the gates of morning ; and a gale sang strong and clean across that pale blue sky which mountains have for a neighbour.

I could see the further valley broadening among woods, to the warmer places; and I went down beside the River Red-cap onwards, whither it pleased me to go.

A FAMILY OF THE FENS

UPON the very limit of the Fens, not a hundred feet in height, but very sharp against the level, there is a lonely little hill. From the edge of that hill the land seems very vague; the flat line of the horizon is the only boundary, and that horizon mixes into watery clouds. No country-side is so formless until one has seen the plan of it set down in a map, but on studying such a map one understands the scheme of the Fens.

The Wash is in the shape of a keystone with the narrow side towards the sea and the broad side towards the land. Imagine the Wash prolonged for twenty or thirty miles inland and broadened considerably as it proceeded as would a curving fan, or better still, a horseshoe, and you have the Fens: a horseshoe whose points, as Dugdale says, are the corners of Lincolnshire and Norfolk.

All around them is land of some little height, and quite dry. It is oolitic on the east, chalky on the south; and the old towns and the old roads look from all round this amphitheatre of dry land down upon the alluvial flats beneath. Peterboro',

Cambridge, Lynn, are all just off the Fens, and the Ermine street runs on the bank which forms their eastern frontier.

This plain has suffered very various fortunes. How good the land was and how well inhabited before the ruin of the monasteries is not yet completely grasped, even by those who love these marshes and who have written their history. Yet there is physical evidence of what was once here ; masses of trees but just buried, grass lying mown in swathes beneath the moss-land, the implements of men where now no men can live, the great buried causeway running right across from east to west.

Beyond such proofs there are the writers who, rare as are the descriptions of medieval scenery, manage to speak of this. For Henry of Huntingdon it was a kind of garden. There were many meres in it, but there were also islands and woods and orchards. William of Malmesbury writes of it with delight, and mentions even its vines. The meres were not impassable marshes ; for instance, in *Domesday* you find the Abbot of Ramsey owning a vessel upon Whittlesea Mere. The whole impression one gets from the earlier time is that of something like the upper waters of the rivers in the Broads : much draining and a good many ponds, but most of the land firm with good deep pastures and a great diversity of woods.

Great catastrophes have certainly overcome this countryside. The greatest was the anarchy of the sixteenth century; but it is probable that, coincidently with every grave lesion in the continuity of our civilization, the Fens suffered, for they always needed the perpetual attention of man to keep them (as they so long were, and may be again if ever our people get back their land and restore a communal life) fully inhabited, afforested, and cultured.

It is probable that the break-up of the ninth century saw the Fens partly drowned, and that after the Black Death something of the same sort happened again, for it is in the latter fourteenth and fifteenth centuries that you begin to hear of a necessity for reclaiming them. John of Gaunt had a scheme, and Morton dug a ditch which is still called "Morton's Leam." I say, every defeat of our civilization was inflicted here in the Fens, but it is certain that the principal disaster followed the suppression of the monasteries.

These great foundations—nourishing hundreds and governing thousands, based upon the populace, drawn from the populace, and living by the common life—were scattered throughout the Fens. They were founded on the "islands" nearest the good land: Thorney, Ramsay, Croyland, Ely—the nuns of Chatteris.

They dated from the very beginning. Ely was

founded within sight of our conversion, 672. Croyland came even before that, before civilization and
religion were truly re-established in Britain;
Penda's great-nephew gave it its charter; St.
Augustine had been dead for little more than
a century when the charter was signed. Even as
the monks came to claim their land they discovered
hermits long settled there. Thorney—Ancarig it
was then—was even fifty years older than Croyland.
The roots of all these go back to the beginning
of the nation.

Ramsay and Chatteris cannot be traced beyond
the gulf of the Danish invasion, but they are
members of the group or ring of houses which
clustered round the edge of the dry land and sent
out its industry towards the Wash, making new
land; for this ring sent out feelers eastward, draining the land and recovering it every way, founding
cells, establishing villages. Holbeach, Spalding,
Freiston, Holland, and I know not how much
more was their land.

When the monasteries were destroyed their
lordship fell into the hands of that high class—
now old, then new—the Cromwells and Russells
and the rest, upon whom has since depended the
greatness of the country. The intensive spirit
proper to a teeming but humble population was
forgotten. The extensive economics of the great
owners, their love of distances and of isolation

took the place of the old agriculture. Within a
generation the whole land was drowned.

The isolated villages forgot the general civilization of England; they came to depend for their
living upon the wildfowl of the marshes; here and
there was a little summer pasturing, more rarely a
little ploughing of the rare patches of dry land; but
the whole place soon ran wild, and there Englishmen soon grew to cause an endless trouble to the
new landlords. These, all the while on from the
death of Henry to that of Elizabeth, pursued their
vigilance and their accumulations. Their power
rose above the marshes like a slow sun and dried
them up at last.

In every inch of England you can find the
history of England. You find it very typically
here. The growth of that leisured class which we
still enjoy—the class that in the seventeenth century destroyed the central government of the
Crown, penetrated and refreshed the universities,
acquired for its use and reformed the endowed
primary education of the English, and began a
thorough occupation of our public land—the
growth of that leisured class is nowhere more
clearly to be seen than in the history of the Fens,
since the Fens had their faith removed from them.

Here is the story of one such family, a family
without whose privileges and public services it
would be difficult to conceive modern England.

Their wealth is rooted in the Fens; the growth of that wealth is parallel to the growth of every fortune by which we are governed.

When the monasteries were despoiled and their farms thrown open to a gamble, when the water ran in again, the countryside and all its generations of human effort were drowned, there was raised up for the restoration of this land the family of Russell.

The Abbey of Thorney had been given to these little squires. They were in possession when, towards the end of Elizabeth's reign, in 1600, was passed the General Draining Act. It was a generous and a broad Act: it was to apply not only to the Great Level, but to all the marshes of the realm. It was soon bent to apply to the family.

Seven years later a Dutchman of the name of Cornelius Vermuyden was sent for, that the work might be begun. For fifty years this man dug and intrigued. He was called in to be the engineer; he had the temerity to compete with the new landlords; he boasted a desire—less legitimate in an alien than in a courtier—to make a great fortune rapidly. He was ruined.

All the adventurers who first attempted the draining of the Fens were ruined—but not that permanent Russell-Francis, the Earl of Bedford, surnamed "the Incomparable."

The story of Vermuyden by him is intricate,

but every Englishman now living on another man's
land should study it. Vermuyden was to drain
the Great Level and to have 95,000 acres for his
pains. These acres were in the occupation—for
the matter of that, in great part the ownership—of
a number of English families. It is true the land
had lain derelict for seventy years, bereft of capital
since the Reformation, and swamped. It is true
that the occupiers (and owners) were very poor.
It is true, therefore, that they could not properly
comprehend a policy that was designed for the
general advantage of the country. They only understood that the hunting and fishing by which
they lived were to stop; that their land was to be
very considerably improved and taken from them.
In their ignorance of ultimate political good they
began to show some considerable impatience.

The cry of the multitude has a way of taking on
the forms of stupidity. The multitude in this case
cried out against Vermuyden. They objected to
a foreigner being given so much freehold. "In
an anguish of despair"—to use one chronicler's
words—"they threw themselves under the protec-
tion of a leader." That leader was, of course,
Francis, Earl of Bedford, surnamed "the Incomparable." He could not hear unmoved the cry of
his fellow-citizens. He yielded to their petition,
took means to oust the Dutchmen, and immediately obtained for himself the grant of the

95,000 acres, by a royal order of 13 January, 1630–31, known as "the Lynn Law."

When he saw the extent of the land and of the water upon it, even his tenacious spirit was alarmed. He therefore associated with himself in the expenses thirteen others, all persons of rank and fortune, as was fitting : alone of the fourteen he preserved his fortune.

The fourteen, then, began the digging of nine drains (if we include the repair of Morton's Leam) ; the largest was that fine twenty-one miles called the old Bedford River, and Charles I, though all in favour of so great a work, was all in dread of the power it might give to the class which—as his prophetic conscience told him—was destined to be his ruin.

There was a contract that the work should be finished in six years : when the six years were ended it was very far from finished. The King grumbled; but Francis, Earl of Bedford, belonged to a clique already half as powerful as the Crown. He threatened, and a new royal order gave him an extension of time. It was the second of his many victories.

The King refused to forget his defeat, and Francis, Earl of Bedford, began to show that hatred of absolute government which has made of his kind the leaders of a happy England. The King did a Stuart thing—he lost his temper. He said, "You may keep your 95,000 acres, but I shall tax them"; and he did. Francis, Earl of Bedford, felt in him a growing passion for just government. He already spoke of freedom; but he had no leisure wherein to enjoy it, for within two years he departed this life, of the small-pox, leaving to his son William the legacy of the great battle for liberty and for the public land.

This change in the Bedford dynasty coincided with the Civil Wars. William Russell, having led some of the Parliamentary forces at Edge Hill, was so uncertain which side might ultimately be victorious as to open secret negotiations with the King. Nothing happened to him, nor even to his brother, who intrigued later against Cromwell's life. He was at liberty to return once more and to survey from the walls of the old abbey the drowned land upon which he had set his heart.

The work of digging could not be carried on during the turmoil of the time; William, Earl of Bedford, filled his leisure in the framing of an elaborate bill of costs. It was dated 20 May, 1646, and showed the sums which he had spent and which had been wasted in the failure to reclaim the Fens. He stated them at over £90,000, and to this he added, like a good business man, interest at the rate of 8 per cent. for so many years as to amount to more than another £30,000.

As against the King, the trick was a good one; but, like many another financier, William, Earl of Bedford, was shortsighted. The more anxious the King grew to pay out public money to the Russells, the less able he grew to do so, till at last he lost not only the shadow of power over the treasury, but life itself; and William, Earl of Bedford, brought in his bill to the Commonwealth.

Cromwell was of the same class, and knew the trick too well. He gave the family leave to prosecute their digging to forget their demand for money. The Act was passed at noon. Bedford was sent for at seven o'clock the next morning and ordered to attend upon Cromwell "and make thankful acknowledgments." He did so.

The works began once more. The common people, in their simplicity, rose as they had so often risen before, against a benefit they could not comprehend; but they no longer had a Stuart to deal with. To their extreme surprise they were put down "with the aid of the military." Then, for all the world as in the promotion of a modern company, the consulting engineer of the original promoters reappears. The Russells had patched it up with Vermuyden, and the work was resumed a third time.

There was, however, this difficulty, that though Englishmen might properly be constrained at this moment to love an orderly and godly life, and to relinquish their property when it was to the public good that they should do so, yet it would have been abhorrent to the whole spirit of the Commonwealth to enslave them even for a work of national advantage. A labour difficulty arose, and the works were in grave peril.

Those whose petty envy may be pleased at the entanglement of William, Earl of Bedford, have forgotten the destiny which maintains our great families. In the worst of the crisis, the battle of Dunbar was fought; 166 Scotch prisoners (and later 500 more) were indentured out to dig the ditches, and it was printed and posted in the end of 1651 that it was "death without mercy" for any to attempt to escape.

The respite was not for long. Heaven, as though to try the patience of its chosen agent, raised up a new obstacle before the great patriot. Peace was made, and the Scotch prisoners were sent home. It was but the passing frown which makes the succeeding smiles of the Deity more gracious. At that very moment Blake was defeating the Dutch upon the seas, and these excellent prisoners, laborious, and (by an accident which clearly shows the finger of Divine providence) especially acquainted with the digging of ditches, arrived in considerable numbers, chained, and handed over to the service of the Premier House.

At the same time it was ordered by the Lord Protector that when the 95,000 acres should at last be dry, any Protestant, even though he were a foreigner, might buy. Two years later an unfortunate peace compelled the return of the Dutch prisoners ; but the work was done, and the Earl of Bedford returned thanks in his cathedral.

Restored to the leisure which is necessary for political action, the Russells actively intrigued for the return of the Stuarts, and pointed out (when Charles II was well upon his throne) how necessary it was for the Fens that their old, if irregular, privileges should be confirmed. It was argued for the Crown that 10,000 acres of land had been quietly absorbed by the Family while there was no king in England : but there happened in this case, what happened in every other since the upper class, the natural leaders of the people, had curbed the tyranny of the King—Charles capitulated. Then followed (of course) popular rising ; it was quelled. Before their long struggle for freedom against the Stuart dynasty was ended, the peasants had been taught their place, Vermuyden was out of the way, the ditches were all dug, the land acquired.

All the world knows the great part played by the House in the emancipation of England from the yoke of James II. The martyrdom of Lord William may have cast upon the Family a passing

cloud ; but whatever compensation the perishable
things of this world can afford, they received and
accepted. In 1694, having assisted at the destruction of yet another form of government, the Earl
of Bedford was made Duke, and on 7 September,
1700, his great work now entirely accomplished,
he departed this life peacefully in his eighty-seventh
year. It was once more in their cathedral that the
funeral sermon was preached by a Dr. Freeman,
chaplain to no less than the King himself. I have
read the sermon in its entirety. It closes with the
fine phrase that William the fifth Earl and the
first Duke of Bedford had sought throughout the
whole of a laborious and patriotic life a crown not
corruptible but incorruptible.

It was precisely a century since the Family had
set out in its quest for that hundred square miles
of land. Through four reigns, a bloody civil war,
three revolutions and innumerable treasons, it had
maintained its purpose, and at last it reached its
goal.

" *Tantæ molis erat Romanam condere gentem.*"

THE ELECTION

THE other day as I was going out upon my travels, I came upon a plain so broad that it greatly wearied me. This plain was grown in parts with barley, but as it stood high in foreign mountains and was arid very little was grown. Small runnels, long run dry under the heat, made the place look like a desert—almost like Africa ; nor was there anything to relieve my gaze except a huddle of small grey houses far away ; but when I reached them I found, to my inexpressible joy, a railway running by and a station to receive me.

For those who complain of railways talk folly, and prove themselves either rich or, more probably, the hangers-on of the rich. A railway is an excellent thing ; it takes one quickly through the world for next to nothing, and if in many countries the people it takes are brutes, and disfigure all they visit, that is not the fault of the railway, but of the Government and religion of these people, which, between them, have ruined the citizens of the State.

So was it not in this place of which I speak, for all the people were industrious, wealthy, kind, amenable and free.

I took a ticket for the only town on the railway list whose history I knew, and then in a third-class carriage made entirely of wood I settled down to a conversation with my kind; for though these people were not of my blood—indeed, I am certain that for some hundreds of years not a drop of their blood has mingled with my own—yet we understood each other by a common tongue called Lingua Franca, of which I have spoken in another place and am a past master.

As all the people round began their talk of cattle, land, and weather, two men next me, or rather the one next me and the other opposite me, began to talk of the election which had been held in that delightful plain : by which, as I learnt, a dealer in herds had been defeated by a somewhat usurious and perhaps insignificant attorney. In this election more than half the voters—that is, a good third of the families in the plain—had gone up to the little huts of wood and had made a mark upon a bit of paper, some on one part, some on the other. About a sixth of the families had desired the dealer in herds to make their laws, and about a sixth the attorney. Of the rest some could not, some would not, go and make the little mark of which I speak. Many more could by law make it, and would have made it, if they had thought it useful to any possible purpose under the sun. One-sixth, I say, had made their mark for the aged and money-lending attorney, and one-sixth for the venerable but avaricious dealer in herds, and since the first sixth was imperceptibly larger than the second it was the lawyer, not the merchant, who stood to make the laws for the people.   But not only to make laws : he was also in some mystic way the Persona and Representative of all the plain.   The long sun-lit fields ; the infinite past—Carolingian, enormous ; the delicate fronds of young trees ; the distant sight of the mountains, which is the note of all that land ; the invasions it had suffered, the conquests it might yet achieve ; its soul and its material self, were all summed up in the solicitor, not in the farmer, and he was to vote on peace or war, on wine or water, on God or no God in the schools.   For the people of the plain were self-governing; they had no lords.

Of my two companions, the one had voted for the cow-buyer, but the other for the scribbler upon parchment, and they discussed their action without heat, gently and with many reasons.

The one said : "It cannot be doubted that the solidarity of society demands that the homogeneity of economic interests should be recognized by the magistrate."   The other said : "The first need is rather that the historic continuity of society should be affirmed by the momentary depositaries of the executive."

For these two men were of some education, and

saw things from a higher standpoint than the peasants around us, who continued to discourse, now angrily, now merrily, but always loudly and rapidly, upon the insignificant matter of their lives: that is, strong, red, bubbling wine, healthy and well-fed beef, rich land and housing, the marriage of daughters, and the putting forward of sons.

Then one of the two, who had long guessed by my dress and face from what country I came, said to me : " And you, how is it in your country ? " I told him we met from time to time, upon occasions not less often than seven years apart, and did just as they had done. That one-sixth of us voted one way and one-sixth the other ; the first, let us say for a money-lender, and the second for a man remarkable for motor-cars or famous for the wealth of his mother ; and whichever sixth was imperceptibly larger than the other, that sixth carried its man, and he stood for the flats of the Wash or for the clear hills of Cumberland, or for Devon, which is all one great and lonely hill.

" This man," said I, " in some very mystic way is *Ourselves*—he is our past and our great national memory. By his vote he decides what shall be done ; but he is controlled."

" By what is he controlled ? " said my companions eagerly. Evidently they had a sneaking love of seeing representatives controlled.

" By a committee of the rich," said I promptly.

At this they shrugged their shoulders and said : "It is a bad system !"

"And by what are yours?" said I.

At this the gravest and oldest of them, looking as it were far away with his eyes, answered : " By the name of our country and a wholesome terror of the people."

"Your system," said I, shrugging my shoulders in turn, but a little awkwardly, "is different from ours."

After this, we were silent all three. We remembered, all three of us, the times when no such things were done in Europe, and yet men hung well together, and a nation was vaguer and yet more instinctive and ready. We remembered also—for it was in our common faith—the gross, permanent, and irremediable imperfection of human affairs. There arose perhaps in their minds a sight of the man they had sent to be the spirit and spokesman, or rather the very self, of that golden plateau which the train was crawling through, and certainly in my mind there rose the picture of a man—small, false, and vile—who was, by some fiction, the voice of a certain valley in my own land.

Then I said to them as I left the train at the town I spoke of : "Days, knights !"—for so one addresses strangers in that country. And they answered : "Your grace, we commend you to God."

ARLES

THE use and the pleasure of travel are closely
mingled, because the use of it is fulfilment, and in fulfilling oneself a great pleasure is
enjoyed. Every man bears within him not only
his own direct experience, but all the past of his
blood: the things his own race has done are part
of himself, and in him also is what his race will
do when he is dead. This is why men will always
read *records*, and why, even when letters are at
their lowest, *records* still remain. Thus, if a diary
be known to be true, then it seems vivid and
becomes famous where if it were fiction no one
would find any merit in it. History, therefore,
once a man has begun to know it, becomes a
necessary food for the mind, without which it
cannot sustain its new dimension. It is an aggre-
gate of universal experience, nor, other things
being equal, is any man's judgment so thin and
weak as the judgment of a man who knows
nothing of the past. But history, if it is to be
kept just and true and not to become a set of airy
scenes, fantastically coloured by our later time,
must be continually corrected and moderated by
the seeing and handling of *things*.

If the West of Europe be one place and one people separate from all the rest of the world, then that unity is of the last importance to us; and that it is so, the wider our learning the more certain we are. All our religion and custom and mode of thought are European. A European State is only a State because it is a State of Europe; and the demarcations between the ever-shifting States of Europe are only dotted lines, but between the Christian and the non-Christian the boundary is hard and full.

Now, a man who recognizes this truth will ask, "Where could I find a model of the past of that Europe? In what place could I find the best single collection of all the forms which European energy has created, and of all the outward symbols in which its soul has been made manifest? To such a man the answer should be given, "You will find these things better in the town of *Arles* than in any other place." A man asking such a question would mean to travel. He ought to travel to *Arles*.

Long before men could write, this hill (which was the first dry land at the head of the Rhone delta, beyond the early mud-flats which the river was pushing out into the sea) was inhabited by our ancestors. Their barbaric huts were grouped round the shelving shore; their axes and their spindles remain.

When thousands of years later the Greeks pushed northward from Massilia, Arles was the first great corner in their road, and the first halting-place after the useless deserts that separated their port from the highway of the Rhone valley.

At the close of Antiquity Rome came to Arles in the beginning of her expansion, and the strong memories of Rome which Arles still holds are famous. Every traveller has heard of the vast unbroken amphitheatre and the ruined temple in a market square that is still called the Forum; they are famous—but when you see them it seems to you that they should be more famous still. They have something about them so familiar and yet so unexpected that the centuries in which they were built come actively before you.

.   .   .   .   .   .

The city of Arles is small and packed. A man may spend an hour in it instead of a day or a year, but in that hour he can receive full communion with antiquity. For as you walk along the tortuous lane between high houses, passing on either hand as you go the ornaments of every age, you turn some dirty little corner or other and come suddenly upon the titanic arches of Rome. There are the huge stones which appal you with the Roman weight and perpetuate in their arrangement an order that has modelled the world. They lie exact and mighty; they are unmoved, clamped with metal, a little worn, enduring. They are none the less a domestic and native part of the living town in which they stand. You pass from the garden of a house that was built in your grandfather's time, and you see familiarly before you in the street a pedestal and a column. They are two thousand years old. You read a placard idly upon the wall; the placard interests you; it deals with the politics of the place or with the army, but the wall might be meaningless. You look more closely, and you see that that wall was raised in a fashion that has been forgotten since the Antonines, and these realities still press upon you, revealed and lost again with every few steps you walk within the limited circuit of the town.

Rome slowly fell asleep. The sculpture lost its power; something barbaric returned. You may see that decline in capitals and masks still embedded in buildings of the fifth century. The sleep grew deeper. There came five hundred years of which so little is left in Europe that Paris has but one doubtful tower and London nothing. Arles still preserves its relics. When Charlemagne was dead and Christendom almost extinguished the barbarian and the Saracen alternately built, and broke against, a keep that still stands and that is still so strong that one might still defend it. It is unlit. It is a dungeon; a ponderous menace above the main street of the city, blind and enormous. It is the very time it comes from.

When all that fear and anarchy of the mind had passed, and when it was discovered that the West still lived, a dawn broke. The medieval civilization began to sprout vigorously through the eleventh and twelfth centuries, as an old tree sprouts before March is out. The memorials of that transition are common enough. We have them here in England in great quantity; we call them the "Norman" architecture. A peculiarly vivid relic of that spring-time remains at Arles. It is the door of what was then the cathedral—the door of St. Trophimus. It perpetuates the beginning of the civilization of the Middle Ages. And of that civilization an accident which has all the force of a particular design has preserved here, attached to this same church, another complete type. The cloisters of this same Church of St. Trophimus are not only the Middle Ages caught and made eternal, they are also a progression of that great experiment from its youth to its sharp close.

You come into these cloisters from a little side street and a neglected yard, which give you no hint of what you are going to see. You find yourself cut off at once and put separately by. Silence inhabits the place; you see nothing but the sky beyond the border of the low roofs. One old man there, who cannot read or write and is all but blind, will talk to you of the Rhone. Then as you go round the arches, "withershins" against the sun (in which way lucky progression has always been made in sacred places), there pass you one after the other the epochs of the Middle Ages. For each group of arches comes later than the last in the order of its sculpture, and the sculptors during those 300 years went withershins as should you.

You have first the solemn purpose of the early work. This takes on neatness of detail, then fineness; a great maturity dignifies all the northern side. Upon the western you already see that spell beneath which the Middle Ages died. The mystery of the fifteenth century; none of its wickedness but all its final vitality, is there. You see in fifty details the last attempt of our race to grasp and permanently to retain the beautiful.

When the circuit is completed the series ends abruptly—as the medieval story itself ended.

There is no way of writing or of telling history which could be so true as these visions are. Arles, at a corner of the great main road of the Empire, never so strong as to destroy nor so insignificant as to cease from building, catching the earliest Roman march into the north, the Christian advance, the full experience of the invasions; retaining in a vague legend the memory of St. Paul; drawing in, after the long trouble, the new life that followed the Crusades, can show such visions better, I think, than Rome herself can show them.

THE GRIFFIN

A SPECIALIST told me once in Ealing that no inn could compare with the Griffin, a Fenland inn. "It is painted green," he said, "and stands in the town of March. If you would enjoy the Griffin, you must ask your way to that town, and as you go ask also for the Griffin, for many who may not have heard of March will certainly have heard of the Griffin."

So I set out at once for the Fens and came at the very beginning of them to a great ditch, which barred all further progress. I wandered up and down the banks for an hour thinking of the inn, when I met a man who was sadder and more silent even than the vast level and lonely land in which he lived. I asked him how I should cross the great dyke. He shook his head, and said he did not know. I asked him if he had heard of the Griffin, but he said no. I broke away from him and went for miles along the bank eastward, seeing the rare trees of the marshes dwindling in the distance, and up against the horizon a distant spire, which I thought might be the Spire of

March.   For March and the Griffin were not twenty
miles away.   And still the great ditch stood between
me and my pilgrimage.

.   .   .   .   .   .

These dykes of the Fens are accursed things:
they are the separation of friends and lovers.
Here is a man whose crony would come and sit by
his fireside at evening and drink with him, a
custom perhaps of twenty years' standing, when
there comes another man from another part armed
with public power, and digs between them a trench
too wide to leap and too soft to ford.   The Fens
are full of such tragedies.

One may march up and down the banks all day
without finding a boat, and as for bridges there
are none, except, indeed, the bridges which the
railway makes ; for the railways have grown to be
as powerful as the landlords or the brewers, and
can go across this country where they choose.
And here the Fens are typical, for it may be said
that these three monopolies—the landlords, the
railways, and the brewers—govern England.

.   .   .   .   .   .

But at last, at a place called Oxlode, I found
a boat, and the news that just beyond lay another
dyke.   I asked where that could be crossed, but
the ferryman of Oxlode did not know.   He pointed
two houses out, however, standing close together
out of the plain, and said that they were called

" Purles' Bridge," and that I would do well to try there. But when I reached them I found that the water was between me and them and, what is more, that there was no bridge there and never had been one since the beginning of time. Of these jests the Fens are full.

In half an hour a man came out of one of the houses and ferried me across in silence. I asked him also if he had heard of the Griffin. He laughed and shook his head as the first one had done, but he showed me a little way off the village of Monea, saying that the people of that place knew every house for a day's walk around. So I trudged to Monea, which is a village on one of the old dry islands of the marsh ; but no one at Monea knew. There was, none the less, one old man who told me he had heard the name, and his advice to me was to go to the cross roads and past them towards March, and then to ask again. So I went outwards to the cross roads, and from the cross roads outward again it seemed without end, a similar land repeating itself for ever. There was the same silence, the same completely even soil, the same deep little trenches, the same rare distant and regular rows of trees.

. . . . . .

Since it was useless to continue thus for you— one yard was as good as twenty miles—and since you could know nothing more of these silences, even if I were to give you every inch of the road, I will pass at once to the moment in which I saw a baker's cart catching me up at great speed. The man inside had an expression of irritable poverty. I did not promise him money, but gave it him. Then he took me aboard and rattled on, with me by his side.

I had by this time a suspicion that the Griffin was a claustral thing and a mystery not to be blurted out. I knew that all the secrets of Hermes may be reached by careful and long-drawn words, and that the simplest of things will not be told one if one asks too precipitately ; so I began to lay siege to his mind by the method of dialogue. The words were these :—

MYSELF : This land wanted draining, didn't it?

THE OTHER MAN : Ah !

MYSELF : It seems to be pretty well drained now.

THE OTHER MAN : Ugh !

MYSELF : I mean it seems dry enough.

THE OTHER MAN : It was drownded only last winter.

MYSELF : It looks to be good land.

THE OTHER MAN : It's lousy land ; it's worth nowt.

MYSELF : Still, there are dark bits—black, you may say—and thereabouts it will be good.

THE OTHER MAN : That's where you're wrong ;

the lighter it is the better it is . . . ah ! that's where many of 'em go wrong. (*Short silence.*)

MYSELF (*cheerfully*) : A sort of loam?

THE OTHER MAN (*Calvinistically*): Ugh!—sand! . . . (*shaking his head*). It blaws away with a blast of wind. (*A longer silence.*)

MYSELF (*as though full of interest*) : Then you set your drills to sow deep about here?

THE OTHER MAN (*with a gesture of fatigue*) : Shoal. (*Here he sighed deeply.*)

After this we ceased to speak to each other for several miles. Then :

MYSELF : Who owns the land about here?

THE OTHER MAN : Some owns parts and some others.

MYSELF (*angrily pointing to an enormous field with a little new house in the middle*) : Who owns that?

THE OTHER MAN (*startled by my tone*): A Frenchman. He grows onions.

Now if you know little of England and of the temper of the English (I mean of ·999 of the English people and not of the ·001 with which you associate), if, I say, you know little or nothing of your fellow-countrymen, you may imagine that all this conversation was wasted. "It was not to the point," you say. "You got no nearer the Griffin." You are wrong. Such conversation is like the kneading of dough or the mixing of mortar; it mollifies and makes ready; it is three-quarters of the work; for if you will let your fellow-citizen curse you and grunt at you, and if you will but talk to him on matters which he knows far better than you, then you have him ready at the end.

So had I this man, for I asked him point-blank at the end of all this: "*What about the Griffin?*" He looked at me for a moment almost with intelligence, and told me that he would hand me over in the next village to a man who was going through March. So he did, and the horse of this second man was even faster than that of the baker. The horses of the Fens are like no horses in the world for speed.

.   .   .   .   .   .

This horse was twenty-three years old, yet it went as fast as though all that tomfoolery men talk about progress were true, and as though things got better by the process of time. It went so fast that one might imagine it at forty-six winning many races, and at eighty standing beyond all comparison or competition; and because it went so fast I went hammering right through the town of March before I had time to learn its name or to know whither I was driving; it whirled me past the houses and out into the country beyond: only when I had pulled up two miles beyond did I know what I had done and did I realize that I had missed for ever one of those

pleasures which, fleeting as they are, are all that is
to be discovered in human life. It went so fast,
that before I knew what had happened the Griffin
had flashed by me and was gone.

. . . . . .

Yet I will affirm with the tongue of faith that
it is the noblest house of call in the Fens.

. . . . . .

It is better to believe than to handle or to see.
I will affirm with the tongue of faith that the
Griffin is, as it were, the captain and chief of these
plains, and has just managed to touch perfection
in all the qualities that an inn should achieve. I
am speaking not of what I know by the doubtful
light of physical experience, but of what I have
seen with the inward eye and felt by something
that transcends gross taste and touch.

Low rooms of my repose! Beams of comfort
and great age; drowsy and inhabiting fires;
ingle-nooks made for companionship. You also,
beer much better, much more soft, than the beer of
lesser towns; beans, bacon, and chicken cooked to
the very limit of excellence; port drawn from
barrels which the simple Portuguese had sent to
Lynn over the cloud-shadowed sea, and honour-
able Lynn without admixture had sent upon a cart
to you, port undefiled, port homogeneous, entirely
made of wine: you also beds! Wooden beds
with curtains around them, feathers for sleeping

on, and every decent thing which the accursed
would attempt to destroy; candles (I trust)—and
trust is more perfect than proof—bread made (if it
be possible) out of English wheat; milk drawn
most certainly from English cows, and butter
worthy of the pastures of England all around.
Oh, glory of the Fens, Griffin, it shall not be said
that I have not enjoyed you!

.   .   .   .   .   .

There is a modern habit, I know, of gloom, and
men without faith upon every side recount the
things that they have not enjoyed.   For my part
I will yield to no such habit.   I will consider that
I have more perfectly tasted in the mind that
which may have been denied to my mere body,
and I will produce for myself and others a greater
pleasure than any pleasure of the sense.   I will do
what the poets and the prophets have always done,
and satisfy myself with vision, and (who knows?)
perhaps by this the Griffin of the Idea has been
made a better thing (if that were possible!) than
the Griffin as it is—as it materially stands in this
evil and uncertain world.

So let the old horse go by and snatch me from
this chance of joy: he has not taken everything
in his flight, and there remains something in spite
of time, which eats us all up.

And yet . . . what is that in me which makes
me regret the Griffin, the real Griffin at which

they would not let me stay? The Griffin painted green : the real rooms, the real fire . . . the material beer? Alas for mortality! Something in me still clings to affections temporal and mundane. England, my desire, what have you not refused me!

THE FIRST DAY'S MARCH

I VERY well remember the spring breaking ten years ago in Lorraine. I remember it better far than I shall ever remember another spring, because one of those petty summits of emotion that seem in boyhood like the peaks of the world was before me. We were going off to camp.

Since every man that fires guns or drives them in France—that is, some hundred thousand and more at any one time, and taking in reserves, half a million—must go to camp in his time, and that more than once, it seems monstrous that a boy should make so much of it; but then to a boy six months is a little lifetime, and for six months I had passed through that great annealing fire of drill which stamps and moulds the French people to-day, putting too much knowledge and bitterness into their eyes, but a great determination into their gestures and a trained tenacity into the methods of their thought.

To me also this fire seemed fiercer and more transforming because, until the day when they had marched me up to barracks in the dark and the rain with the batch of recruits, I had known nothing but the easy illusions and the comfort of an English village, and had had but journeys or short visits to teach me that enduring mystery of Europe, the French temper : whose aims and reticence, whose hidden enthusiasms, great range of effort, divisions, defeats, and resurrections must now remain the principal problem before my mind; for the few who had seen this sight know that the French mind is the pivot on which Europe turns.

I had come into the regiment faulty in my grammar and doubtful in accent, ignorant especially of those things which in every civilization are taken for granted but never explained in full; I was ignorant, therefore, of the key which alone can open that civilization to a stranger. Things irksome or a heavy burden to the young men of my age, born and brought up in the French air, were to me, brought up with Englishmen an Englishman, odious and bewildering. Orders that I but half comprehended; simple phrases that seemed charged with menace; boasting (a habit of which I knew little), coupled with a fierce and, as it were, expected courage that seemed ill-suited to boasting—and certainly unknown outside this army; enormous powers of endurance in men whose stature my English training had taught me to despise ; a habit of fighting with the fists, coupled with a curious contempt for the accident of individual superiority—all these things amazed me and put me into a topsy-turvy world where I was weeks in finding my feet.

But strangest of all, and (as I now especially believe) most pregnant with meaning for the future, was to find the inherited experience in me of so much teaching and careful habit—instinct of command, if you will—all that goes to make what we call in Western Europe a " gentleman," put at the orders and the occasional insult of a hierarchy of office, many of whose functionaries were peasants and artisans.   Stripes on the arm, symbols, suddenly became of overwhelming value ; what I had been made with so much care in an English public school was here thought nothing but a hindrance and an absurdity.   This had seemed to me first a miracle, then a grievous injustice, then most unpractical, and at last, like one that sees the answer to a riddle, I saw (when I had long lost my manners and ceased to care for refinements) that the French were attempting, a generation before any others in the world, to establish an army that should be a mere army, and in which a living man counted only as one numbered man.

Whether that experiment will hold or not I cannot tell ; it shocks the refinement of the whole West of Europe ; it seems monstrous to the aristocratic organization of Germany; it jars in France also with the traditions of that decent elder class of whom so many still remain to guide the Republic, and in whose social philosophy the segregation of a "directing class" has been hitherto a dogma. But soon I cared little whether that experiment was to succeed or no in its final effort, or whether the French were to perfect a democracy where wealth has one vast experience of its own artificiality, or to fail. The intellectual interest of such an experiment, when once I seized it, drove out every other feeling.

I became like a man who has thoroughly awaked from a long sleep and finds that in sleep he has been taken overseas. I merged into the great system whose wheels and grindings had at first astonished or disgusted me, and I found that they had made of me what they meant to make. I cared more for guns than for books; I now obeyed by instinct not men, but symbols of authority. No comfortable fallacy remained; it no longer seemed strange that my captain was a man promoted from the ranks; that one of my lieutenants was an Alsatian charity boy and the other a rich fellow mixed up with sugar-broking; that the sergeant of my piece should be a poor young noble, the wheeler of No. 5 a wealthy and very vulgar chemist's son, the man in the next bed (my "ancient," as they say in that service) a cook of some skill, and my bombardier a mild young farmer. I thought only in terms of the artillery : I could judge men for their aptitude alone, and in me, I suppose, were accomplished many things— one of Danton's dreams, one of St. Just's prophecies, the fulfilment also of what a hundred brains had silently determined twenty years before when the staff gave up their swords outside Metz ; the army and the kind of army of which Chanzy had said in the first breath of the armistice, " A man who forgets it should be hanged, but a man who speaks of it before its time should be shot with the honours of his rank."

All this had happened to me in especial in that melting-pot up in the eastern hills, and to thirty thousand others that year in their separate crucibles.

In the process things had passed which would seem to you incredible if I wrote them all down. I cared little in what vessel I ate, or whether I had to tear meat with my fingers. I could march in reserve more than twenty miles a day for day upon day. I knew all about my horses ; I could sweep, wash, make a bed, clean kit, cook a little, tidy a stable, turn to entrenching for emplacement, take a place at lifting a gun or changing a wheel. I took change with a gunner, and could point well. And all this was not learnt save under a grinding pressure of authority and harshness, without which in one's whole life I suppose one would never properly have learnt a half of these things—at least, not to do them so readily, or in such unison, or on so definite a plan. But (what will seem astonishing to our critics and verbalists) with all this there increased the power, or perhaps it was but the desire, to express the greatest thoughts—newer and keener things. I began to understand De Vigny when he wrote, "If a man despairs of becoming a poet, let him carry his pack and march in the ranks."

Thus the great hills that border the Moselle, the distant frontier, the vast plain which is (they say) to be a battlefield, and which lay five hundred feet sheer below me; the far guns when they were practising at Metz, the awful strength of columns on the march moved me. The sky also grew more wonderful, and I noticed living things. The Middle Ages, of which till then I had had but troubling visions, rose up and took flesh in the old town, on the rare winter evenings when I had purchased the leisure to leave quarters by some excessive toil. A man could feel France going by.

It was at the end of these six months, when there was no more darkness at roll-call, and when the bitter cold (that had frozen us all winter) was half forgotten, that the spring brought me this excellent news, earlier than I had dared to expect it—the news that sounds to a recruit half as good as active service. We were going to march and go off right away westward over half a dozen horizons, till we could see the real thing at Chalons, and with this news the world seemed recreated.

Seven times that winter we had been mobilized ; four times in the dead of the night, once at mid-day, once at evening, and once at dawn. Seven times we had started down the wide Metz road, hoping in some vague way that they would do something with us and give us at least some manœuvres, and seven times we had marched back to barracks to undo all that serious packing and to return to routine.

Once, for a week in February, the French and German Governments, or, more probably, two minor permanent officials, took it into their silly heads that there was some danger of war. We packed our campaign saddles every night and put them on the pegs behind the stalls ; we had the emergency rations served out, and for two days in the middle of that time we had slept ready. But nothing came of it. Now at least we were off to play a little at the game whose theory we had learnt so wearily.

And the way I first knew it would easily fill a book if it were told as it should be, with every detail and its meaning unrolled and with every joy described: as it is, I must put it in ten lines. Garnon (a sergeant), three others, and I were sent

out (one patrol out of fifty) to go round and see
the reserve horses on the farms. That was delight
enough, to have a vigorous windy morning with
the clouds large and white and in a clear sky, and
to mix with the first grain of the year, "out of the
loose-box."

We took the round they gave us along the base
of the high hills, we got our papers signed at the
different stables, we noted the hoofs of the horses
and their numbers; a good woman at a large farm
gave us food of eggs and onions, and at noon we
turned to get back to quarters for the grooming.
Everything then was very well—to have ridden
out alone without the second horse and with no
horrible great pole to crush one's leg, and be
free—though we missed it—of the clank of the
guns. We felt like gentlemen at ease, and were
speaking grandly to each other, when I heard
Garnon say to the senior of us a word that made
things seem better still, for he pointed out to a
long blue line beyond Domremy and overhanging
the house of Joan of Arc, saying that the town lay
there. "What town?" said I to my Ancient; and
my Ancient, instead of answering simply, took five
minutes to explain to me how a recruit could
not know that the round of the reserve horses
came next before camp, and that this town away
on the western ridge was the first halting-place
upon the road. Then my mind filled with distances,

and I was overjoyed, saving for this one thing, that I had but two francs and a few coppers left, and that I was not in reach of more.

When we had ridden in, saluted and reported at the guard, we saw the guns drawn up in line at the end of the yard, and we went into grooming and ate and slept, hardly waiting for the morning and the long regimental call before the réveillé; the notes that always mean the high road for an army, and that are as old as Fontenoy.

.   .   .   .   .   .

That next morning they woke us all before dawn—long before dawn. The sky was still keen, and there was not even a promise of morning in the air, nor the least faintness in the eastern stars. They twinkled right on the edges of the world over the far woods of Lorraine, beyond the hollow wherein lay the town ; it was even cold like winter as we harnessed ; and I remember the night air catching me in the face as I staggered from the harness-room, with my campaign saddle and the traces and the girths and the saddle cloth, and all the great weight that I had to put upon my horses.

We stood in the long stables all together, very hurriedly saddling and bridling and knotting up the traces behind. A few lanterns gave us an imperfect light. We hurried because it was a pride to be the first battery, and in the French service, rightly or wrongly, everything in the artillery is made for speed, and to speed everything is sacrificed. So we made ready in the stable and brought our horses out in order before the guns in the open square of quarters. The high plateau on which the barracks stood was touched with a last late frost, and the horses coming out of the warm stables bore the change ill, lifting their heads and stamping. A man could not leave the leaders for a moment, and, while the chains were hooked on, even my middle horses were restive and had to be held. My hands stiffened at the reins, and I tried to soothe both my beasts, as the lantern went up and down wherever the work was being done. They quieted when the light was taken round behind by the tumbrils, where two men were tying on the great sack of oats exactly as though we were going on campaign.

These two horses of mine were called Pacte and Basilique. Basilique was saddled : a slow beast, full of strength and sympathy, but stupid and given to sudden fears. Pacte was the led horse, and had never heard guns. It was prophesied that when first I should have to hold him in camp when we were practising he would break everything near him, and either kill me or get me cells. But I did not believe these prophecies, having found my Ancient and all third-year men too often to be liars, fond of frightening the younger recruits. Meanwhile Pacte stood in the sharp night, impatient, and shook his harness. Everything had been quickly ordered.

We filed out of quarters, passed the lamp of the guard, and saw huddled there the dozen or so that were left behind while we were off to better things. Then a drawn-out cry at the head of the column was caught up all along its length, and we trotted ; the metal of shoes and wheel-rims rang upon the road, and I felt as a man feels on a ship when it leaves harbour for great discoveries.

We had climbed the steep bank above St. Martin, and were on the highest ridge of land dominating the plain, when the sky first felt the approach of the sun. Our backs were to the east, but the horizon before us caught a reflection of the dawn ; the woods lost their mystery, and one found oneself marching in a partly cultivated open space with a forest all around. The road ran straight for miles like an arrow, and stretched swarmingly along it was the interminable line of guns. But with the full daylight, and after the sun had risen in a mist, they deployed us out of column into a wide front on a great heath in the forest, and we halted. There we brewed coffee, not by batteries, but gun by gun.

Warmed by this little meal, mere coffee without sugar or milk, but with a hunk left over from yes-

terday's bread and drawn stale from one's haver-
sack (the armies of the Republic and of Napoleon
often fought all day upon such sustenance, and
even now, as you will see, the French do not
really eat till a march is over—and this may be a
great advantage in warfare)—warmed, I say, by
this little meal, and very much refreshed by the
sun and the increasing merriment of morning, we
heard first the trumpet-call and then the shouted
order to mount.

We did not form one column again. We went
off at intervals by batteries; and the reason of this
was soon clear, for on getting to a place where
four roads met, some took one and some took
another, the object being to split up the unwieldy
train of thirty-six guns, with all their waggons
and forges, into a number of smaller groups,
marching by ways more or less parallel towards
the same goal; and my battery was left separate,
and went at last along a lane that ran through
pasture land in a valley.

The villages were already awake, and the mist
was all but lifted from the meadows when we
heard men singing in chorus in front of us some
way off. These were the gunners that had left
long before us and had gone on forward afoot.
For in the French artillery it is a maxim (for all I
know, common to all others—if other artilleries
are wise) that you should weight your limber (and

therefore your horses) with useful things alone ; and as gunners are useful only to fire guns, they are not carried, save into action or when some great rapidity of movement is desired.   I do, indeed, remember one case when it was thought necessary to send a group of batteries during the manœuvres right over from the left to the right of a very long position which our division was occupying on the crest of the Argonne.   There was the greatest need for haste, and we packed the gunners on to the limber (there were no seats on the gun in the old type—there are now) and galloped all the way down the road, and put the guns in action with the horses still panting and exhausted by that extra weight carried at such a speed and for such a distance.   But on the march, I say again, we send the gunners forward, and not only the gunners, but, as you shall hear when we come to Commercy, a reserve of drivers also. We send them forward an hour or two before the guns start ; we catch them up with the guns on the road ; they file up to let us pass, and commonly salute us by way of formality and ceremony.   Then they come into the town of the halt an hour or two after we have reached it.

So here in this silent and delightful valley, through which ran a river, which may have been the Meuse or may have been a tributary only, we caught up our gunners.   Their song ceased, they were lined up along the road, and not till we were passed were they given a little halt and repose. But when we had gone past with a huge clattering and dust, the bombardier of my piece, who was a very kindly man, a young farmer, and who happened to be riding abreast of my horses, pointed them out to me behind us at a turning in the road. They were taking that five minutes' rest which the French have borrowed from the Germans, and which comes at the end of every hour on the march. They had thrown down their knapsacks and were lying flat taking their ease. I could not long look backwards, but a very little time after, when we had already gained nearly half a mile upon them, we again heard the noise of their singing, and knew that they had re-shouldered the heavy packs. And this pack is the same in every unmounted branch of the service, and is the heaviest thing, I believe, that has been carried by infantry since the Romans.

It was not yet noon, and extremely hot for the time of year and for the coldness of the preceding night, when they halted us at a place where the road bent round in a curve and went down a little hollow. There we dismounted and cleaned things up a little before getting into the town, where we were to find what the French call an *étape;* that is, the town at which one halts at the end of one's march, and the word is also used for the length of

a march itself. It is not in general orders to clean
up in this way before coming in, and there were
some commanders who were never more pleased
than when they could bring their battery into town
covered with dust and the horses steaming and the
men haggard, for this they thought to be evidence
of a workmanlike spirit. But our colonel had given
very contrary orders, to the annoyance of our
captain, a man risen from the ranks who loved the
guns and hated finery.

Then we went at a walk, the two trumpets of the
battery sounding the call which is known among
French gunners as "the eighty hunters," because
the words to it are, "*quatre-vingt, quatre-vingt,
quatre-vingt, quatre-vingt, quatre-vingt, quatre-
vingt, quatre-vingt, chasseurs,*" which words, by
their metallic noise and monotony, exactly express
the long call that announces the approach of guns.
We went right through the town, the name of
which is Commercy, and the boys looked at us
with pride, not knowing how hateful they would
find the service when once they were in for its
grind and hopelessness. But then, for that matter,
I did not know myself with what great pleasure I
should look back upon it ten years after. Moreover, nobody knows beforehand whether he will
like a thing or not ; and there is the end of it.

We formed a park in the principal place of the
town ; there were appointed two sentinels to do

duty until the arrival of the gunners who should relieve them and mount a proper guard, and then we were marched off to be shown our various quarters. For before a French regiment arrives at a town others have ridden forward and have marked in chalk upon the doors how many men and how many horses are to be quartered here or there, and my quarters were in a great barn with a very high roof; but my Ancient, upon whom I depended for advice, was quartered in a house, and I was therefore lonely.

We groomed our horses, ate our great mid-day meal, and were free for a couple of hours to wander about the place. It is a garrison, and, at that time, it was full of cavalry, with whom we fraternized ; but the experiment was a trifle dangerous, for there is always a risk of a quarrel when regiments meet as there is with two dogs, or two of any other kind of lively things.

Then came the evening, and very early, before it was dark, I was asleep in my clothes in some straw, very warm; but I was so lazy that I had not even taken off my belt or sword. And that was the end of the first day's marching.

THE SEA-WALL OF THE WASH

THE town of Wisbeach is very like the town of Boston. It stands upon a river which is very narrow and which curves, and in which there rises and falls a most considerable tide, and which is bounded by slimy wooden sides. Here, as at Boston, the boats cannot turn round ; if they come in frontways they have to go out backwards, like Mevagissey bees : an awkward harbour.

As I sat there in the White Hart, waiting for steak and onions, I read in a book descriptive of the place that a whale had come to Wisbeach once, and I considered that a whale coming up to Wisbeach on a tide would certainly stay there ; not indeed for the delights of the town (of which I say nothing), but because there would be no room for it to turn round ; and a whale cannot swim backwards. The only fish that can swim backwards is an eel. This I have proved by observation, and I challenge any fisherman to deny it.

So much for Wisbeach, which stands upon the River Nene or Nen, which is the last of the towns defended by the old sea-wall—which is the third of the Fen ports—the other two being Boston and Lynn, which is served by two lines of railway and which has two stations.

Very early next morning, and by one of these stations, another man and I took train to a bridge called Sutton Bridge, where one can cross the River Nen, and where (according to the map) one can see both the sea-walls, the old and the new. It was my plan to walk along the shore of the Wash right across the flats to Lynn, and so at last perhaps comprehend the nature of this curious land.

.   .   .   .   .   .

When I got to Sutton Bridge I discovered it to be a monstrous thing of iron standing poised upon a huge pivot in mid-stream. It bore the railway and the road together. It was that kind of triumphant engineering which once you saw only in England, but which now you will see all over the world. It was designed to swing open on its central pivot to let boats go up the River Nen, and then to come back exactly to its place with a clang ; but when we got to it we found it neither one thing nor the other. It was twisted just so much that the two parts of the roads (the road on the bridge and the road on land) did not join.

Was a boat about to pass ? No. Why was it open thus ? A man was cleaning it. The bridge is not as big as the Tower Bridge, but it is very big, and the man was cleaning it with a little rag. He was cleaning the under part, the mechanisms and contraptions that can only be got at when the bridge is thus ajar. He cleaned without haste and without exertion, and as I watched him I considered the mightiness of the works of Man contrasted with His Puny Frame. I also asked him when I should pass, but he answered nothing.

As we thus waited men gathered upon either side—men of all characters and kinds, men holding bicycles, men in carts, afoot, on horseback, vigorous men and feeble, old men, women also and little children, and youths witless of life, and innocent young girls; they gathered and increased, they became as numerous as leaves, they stretched out their hands in a desire for the further shore : but the river ran between.

Then, as being next the gate, I again called out: When might we pass? A Fenland man who was on duty there doing nothing said, I could pass when the bridge was shut again. I said : When would that be? He said : Could I not see that the man was cleaning the bridge? I said that, contrasting the bridge with him and his little rag, he might go on from now to the Disestablishment of the English Church before he had done ; but as for me, I desired to cross, and so did all that multitude.

Without grace they shut the bridge for us, the gate opened of itself, and in a great clamorous flood, like an army released from a siege, we poured over, all of us, rejoicing into Wringland ; for so is called this flat, reclaimed land, which stands isolated between the Nen and the Ouse.

．　　．　　．　　．　　．　　．

Was I not right in saying when I wrote about Ely that the corner of a corner of England is infinite, and can never be exhausted ?

Along the cut which takes the Nen out to sea, then across some level fields, and jumping a ditch or two, one gets to the straight, steep, and high dyke which protects the dry land and cuts off the plough from the sea marshes. When I had climbed it and looked out over endless flats to the sails under the brune of the horizon I understood the Fens.

．　　．　　．　　．　　．　　．

Nowhere that I have been to in the world does the land fade into the sea so inconspicuously.

The coasts of western England are like the death of a western man in battle—violent and heroic. The land dares all, and plunges into a noisy sea. This coast of eastern England is like the death of one of these eastern merchants here—lethargic, ill-contented, drugged with ease.   The dry land slips, and wallows into a quiet, very shallow water, confused with a yellow thickness and brackish with the weight of inland water behind.

I have heard of the great lakes, especially of the marshes at the mouth of the Volga, in the Caspian, where the two elements are for miles indistinguishable, and where no one can speak of a shore ; but here the thing is more marvellous, because it is the true sea. You have, I say, the true sea, with great tides, and bearing ships, and seaports to which the ships can go ; and on the other side you have, inhabited, an ancient land. There should be a demarcation between them, a tide mark or limit. There is nothing. You cannot say where one begins and the other ends. One does not understand the Fens until one has seen that shore.

The sand and the mud commingle. The mud takes on little tufts of salt grass barely growing under the harsh wind. The marsh is cut and wasted into little islands covered at every high tide, except, perhaps, the extreme of the neaps. Down on that level, out from the dyke to the uncertain line of the water, you cannot walk a hundred yards without having to cross a channel more or less deep, a channel which the working of the muddy tides has scoured up into the silt and ooze of the sodden land. These channels are yards deep in slime, and they ramify like the twisted shoots of an old vine. Were you to make a map of them as they engrave this desolate waste

it would look like the fine tortuous cracks that
show upon antique enamel, or the wandering of
threads blown at random on a woman's work-
table by the wind.

There are miles and miles of it right up to the
EMBANKMENT, the great and old SEA-WALL which
protects the houses of men. You have but to
eliminate that embankment to imagine what the
whole countryside must have been like before it
was raised, and the meaning of the Fens becomes
clear to you. The Fens were long ago but the
continuation inland of this sea-morass. The tide
channels of the marsh were all of one kind, though
they differed so much in size. Some of these
channels were small without name; some a little
larger, and these had a local name; others were a
little larger again, and worthy to be called rivers—
the Ouse, the Nen, the Welland, the Glen, the
Witham. But, large or small, they were nothing,
all of them, but the scouring of tide-channels in
the light and sodden slime. It was the high tide
that drowned all this land, the low tide that drained
it; and wherever a patch could be found just
above the influence of the tide or near enough to
some main channel for the rush and swirl of the
water to drain the island, there the villages grew.
Wherever such a patch could be found men built
their first homes. Sometimes, before men civic,
came the holy hermits. But man, religious, or

greedy, or just wandering, crept in after each inundation and began to tame the water and spread out even here his slow, interminable conquest.   So Wisbeach, so March, so Boston grew, and so—the oldest of them all—the Isle of Ely.

The nature of the country (a nature at which I had but guessed whenever before this I had wandered through it, and which I had puzzled at as I viewed its mere history) was quite clear, now that I stood upon the wall that fenced it in from the salt water.   It was easy to see not only what judgments had been mistaken, but also in what way they had erred.   One could see how and why the homelessness of the place had been exaggerated.   One could see how the level was just above (not, as in Holland, below) the mean of the tides. One could discover the manner in which communication from the open sea was possible.   The deeps lead out through the sand ; they are but continuations under water of that tide-scouring which is the note of all the place inland, and out, far out, we could see the continuation of the river-beds, and at their mouths, far into the sea, the sails.

A man sounding as he went before the northeast wind was led by force into the main channels. He was "shepherded" into Lynn River or Wisbeach River or Boston River, according as he found the water shoaler to one side or other of his boat.   So must have come the first Saxon pirates from the mainland; so (hundreds of years later) came here our portion of that swarm of Pagans, which all but destroyed Europe; so centuries before either of them, in a time of which there is no record, the ignorant seafaring men from the east and the north must have come right up into our island, as the sea itself creeps right up into the land through these curious crevices and draughts in the Fenland wall.

Men—at least the men of our race—have made everything for themselves; and they will never cease. They continue to extend and possess. It is not only the architecture; it is the very landscape of Europe which has been made by Europeans. In what way did we begin to form this difficult place, which is neither earth nor water, and in which we might have despaired? It was conquered by human artifice, of course, somewhat as Frisia and the Netherlands, and, as we may believe, the great bay of the Cotentin were conquered; but it has certain special characters of its own, and these again are due to the value in this place of the tides, and to the absence of those natural dykes of sand which were, a thousand years ago, the beginnings of Holland.

· · · · · ·

Two methods, working side by side, have from the beginning of human habitation reclaimed the

Fens. The first has been the canalization, the fencing in of the tideways; the second has been the banking out of the general sea. The spring tides covered much of this land, and when they retired left it drowned. Against their universal advancing sheet of water a bank could be made. Such a bank cut off the invasion of the hundreds of runnels, small and great, by which the more ordinary tides that could not cover the surface had yet crept into the soil and soaked it through.

When such a bank had been built, gates, as it were, permitted the water to spend its force and also to use its ebb and flow for the draining of the land beyond. The gates which let the tide pour up and down the main ways became the new mouths of the main rivers; inland the course of the rivers (which now took all the sea and thus became prodigious) were carefully guarded. Even before trenches were dug to drain the fields around, earth was thrown up on either side of the rivers to confine them each to one permanent channel; nor did the level of the rivers rise, or their beds get clogged; the strength of the tide sufficed for the deepening of their channels. Into the rivers so fortified the other waterways of the Fens were conducted.

By these methods alone much of the land was rendered habitable and subject to the plough. Probably these methods were enough to make it all it was in the Middle Ages. It was only far later, almost in our own time, that water was gathered by trenches in the lowland beneath the rivers and pumped out artificially with mills ; nor is it quite certain even now that this method (borrowed from Holland) is the best ; for the land, as I have said, is above and not below the sea.

Of these works, whose tradition is immemorial, the greatest, of course, are the sea-walls.

Perhaps the river-walls came first, but the great bank which limited and protected the land against the sea is also older than any history.

It is called Roman, and relics of Rome have been found in it, but it has not the characteristic of Roman work. It runs upon no regular lines ; its contour is curved and variable. It is surely far older than the Roman occupation. Earth, heaped and beaten hard, is the most enduring of things ; the tumuli all over England have outlasted even the monoliths, and the great defensive mounds at Norwich and at Oxford are stronger and clearer cut than anything that the Middle Ages have left. This bank, which first made Fenland, still stands most conspicuous. You may follow it from the Nene above Sutton Bridge right over to Lynn River, and again northward from Sutton Bridge (or rather, from the ferry above it) right round *outside* Long Sutton and Holbeach, and by Fors-dyke Bridge and *outside* Swyneshead ; everywhere it encloses and protects the old parishes, and everywhere seaward of it the names of the fields mark the newest of endeavours.

.   .   .   .   .   .

We returned from a long wandering upon the desolate edges of the sea to the bank which we proposed to follow right round to the mouth of the Ouse : a bank that runs not straight, but in great broken lines, as in old-fashioned fortification, and from which far off upon the right one sees the famous churches of the Wringland, far off upon the left a hint beyond the marshes and the sands of the very distant open sea.

A gale had risen with the morning, and while it invigorated the travellers in these wastes it seemed to increase their loneliness, for it broke upon nothing, and it removed the interest of the eye from the monotonous sad land to the charge and change of the torn sky above, but in a sense also it impelled us, as though we were sailing before it as it swept along the edge of the bank and helped us to forget the interminable hours.

The birds for whom this estuary is a kind of sanctuary and a place of secure food in all weathers, the birds swept out in great flocks over the flats towards the sea.   They were the only companion-ship afforded to us upon this long day, and they had, or I fancied they had, in their demeanour a kind of contempt for the rare human beings they might see, as though knowing how little man could do upon those sands. They fed all together upon the edge of the water, upon the edge of the falling tide, very far off, making long bands of white that mixed with the tiny breaking wavelets. Now and then they rose in bodies, and so rising disappeared; but as they would turn and wheel against the wind, seeking some other ground, they sent from moment to moment flashes of delicate and rare light from the great multitude of their wings. I know of nothing to which one may compare these glimpses of evanescent shining but these two things —the flash of a sword edge and the rapid turning in human hands of a diaphanous veil held in the light. It shone or glinted for a moment, then they would all wheel together and it disappeared.

So, watching them as a kind of marvel, we saw distant across the sea a faint blue tower, and recognized it for Boston Stump, so many, many miles away.

But for the birds and this landmark, which never left us, all the length of the dyke was empty of any sight save the mixing of the sea and the land. Then gradually the heights in Norfolk beyond grew clearer, a further shore narrowed the expanse of waters, and we came to the river mouth of the Ouse, and caught sight, up the stream, of the houses of a town.

THE CERDAGNE

THERE is a part of Europe of which for the moment most people have not heard, but which in a few years everybody will know; so it is well worth telling before it is changed what it is like to-day. It is called the Cerdagne. It is a very broad valley, stretching out between hills whose height is so incredible—or at least, whose appearance of height is so incredible—that when they are properly painted no one will believe them to be true. Indeed, I know a man who painted them just as they are, and those who saw the picture said it was fantastic and out of Nature, like Turner's drawings. But those who had been with him and had seen the place, said that somehow he had just missed the effect of height.

It is remarkable that in any country, even if one does not know that country well, what is unusual to the country strikes the traveller at once. And so it is with the Cerdagne. For all the valleys of the Pyrenees except this one are built upon the same plan. They are deep gorges, narrowing in two places to gates or profound

corridors, one of these places being near the
crest and one near the plain; and down these
valleys fall violent torrents, and in them there is
only room for tiny villages or very little towns,
squeezed in between the sheer surfaces of the rock
or the steep forests.

So it is with the Valley of Laruns, and with
that of Meuléon, and with that of Luz, and with
those of the two Bagnères, and with the Val d'Aran,
and with the Val d'Esera, and with the very famous
Valley of Andorra.

With valleys so made the mountains are indeed
more awful than they might be in the Alps; but
you never see them standing out and apart, and the
mastering elevation of the Pyrenees is not appre-
hended until you come to the cirque or hollow at
the end of each valley just underneath the main
ridge; by that time you have climbed so far that
you have halved the height of the barrier.

But the Cerdagne, unlike all the other valleys,
is as broad as half a county, and is full of towns
and fields and men and mules and slow rivulets
and corn; so, standing upon either side and looking to the other, you see all together and in
the large its mountain boundaries. It is like the
sight of the Grampians from beyond Strathmore,
but very much more grand. Moreover, as no one
has written sufficiently about it to prepare the
traveller for what he is to see (and in attempting

to do so here I am probably doing wrong, but
a man must write down what he has seen), the
Cerdagne breaks upon him quite unexpectedly, and
his descent into that wealthy plain is the entry into
a new world. He may have learnt the mountains
by heart, as we had, in many stumbling marches
and many nights slept out beneath the trees, and
many crossings of the main chain by those precipitous cols which make the ridge of the Pyrenees
more like a paling than a mountain crest. But
though he should know them thoroughly all the
way from the Atlantic for two hundred miles, the
Cerdagne will only appear to him the more astonishing. It renews in any man, however familiar
he may be with great mountains, the impressions
of that day when he first saw the distant summits
and thought them to be clouds.

Apart from all this, the Cerdagne is full of a
lively interest, because it preserves far better than
any other Pyrenean valley those two Pyrenean
things—the memory of European history and the
intense local spirit of the Vals.

The memory of European history is to be seen
in the odd tricks which the frontier plays. It was
laid down by the commissioners of Mazarin two
hundred and fifty years ago, and instead of following the watershed (which would leave the Cerdagne
all Spanish politically as it is Catalan by language
and position) it crosses the valley from one side to

another, leaving the top end of it and the sources of its rivers under French control.

That endless debate as to whether race or government will most affect a people can here be tested, though hardly decided. The villages are Spanish, the hour of meals is Spanish, and the wine is Spanish wine. But the clocks keep time, and the streets are swept, and, oddest of all, the cooking is French cooking. The people are Spanish in that they are slow to serve you or to find you a mount or to show you the way, but they are French in that they are punctual in the hour at which they have promised to do these things; and they are Spanish in the shapes of their ricks and the nature of their implements, but French in the aspect of their fields. One might also discuss—it would be most profitable of all—where they are Spanish and where they are French in their observance of religion.

This freak which the frontier plays in cutting so united a countryside into two by an imaginary line is further emphasized by an island of Spanish territory which has been left stranded, as it were, in the midst of the valley. It is called Llivia, and is about as large as a large English country parish, with a small country town in the middle.

One comes across the fields from villages where the signs and villagers and the very look of the surface of the road are French; one suddenly notices Spanish soldiers, Spanish signs, and Spanish prices in the streets of the little place; one leaves it, and in five minutes one is in France again. It is connected with its own country by a neutral road, but it is an island of territory all the same, and the reason that it was so left isolated is very typical of the spirit of the old regime, with its solemn legal pedantry, which we in England alone preserve in all Western Europe. For the treaty which marked the limits here ceded to the French "the valley and all its villages." The Spaniards pleaded that Llivia was not a village but a town, and their plea was admitted.

I began by saying that this wide basin of land, with its strong people and its isolated traditions, though it was so little known to-day, would soon be too well known. So it will be, and the reason is this, that the very low pass at one end of it will soon be crossed by a railway. It is the only low pass in the Pyrenees, and it is so gradual and even (upon the Spanish side) that the railway will everywhere be above ground. Within perhaps five years it will be for the Pyrenees what the Brenner is for the Alps, and when that is done any one who has read this may go and see for himself whether it is not true that from that plain at evening the frontier ridge of Andorra seems to be the highest thing in the world.

CARCASSONNE

CARCASSONNE differs from other monumental towns in this : that it preserves exactly the aspect of many centuries up to a certain moment, and from that moment has " set," and has suffered no further change. You see and touch, as you walk along its ramparts, all the generations from that crisis in the fifth century when the public power was finally despaired of—and after which each group of the Western Empire began to see to its own preservation—down to that last achievement of the thirteenth, when medieval civilization had reached its full flower and was ready for the decline that followed the death of St. Louis and the extinction of the German phantasy of empire.

No other town can present so vivid and clean-cut a fossil of the seven hundred years into which poured and melted all the dissolution of antiquity, and out of which was formed or crystallized the highly specialized diversity of our modern Europe.

In the fascination of extreme age many English sites are richer; Winchester and Canterbury may be quoted from among a hundred. In the superimposition of age upon age of human history,

Arles and Rome are far more surprising. In historic continuity most European towns surpass it, from Paris, whose public justice, worship, and markets have kept to the same site for quite sixteen centuries, to London, of which the city at least preserves upon three sides the Roman limit. But no town can of its nature give as does Carcassonne this overwhelming impression of survival or resurrection.

The attitude and position of Carcassonne enforce its character. Up above the river, but a little set back from the valley, right against the dawn as you come to it from Toulouse through the morning, stands a long, steep, and isolated rock, the whole summit of which from the sharp cliff on the north to that other on the south is doubled in height by what seems one vast wall—and more than twenty towers. Indeed, it is at such a time, in early morning, and best in winter when the frost defines and chisels every outline, that Carcassonne should be drawn. You then see it in a band of dark blue-grey, all even in texture, serrated and battlemented and towered, with the metallic shining of the dawn behind it.

So to have seen it makes it very difficult to write of it or even to paint; what one wishes to do is rather to work it out in enamel upon a surface of bronze. This rock, wholly covered with the works of the city, stands looking at the Pyrenees and holding the only level valley between the Mediterranean and the Garonne, and even if one had read nothing concerning it one would understand why it has filled all the legends of the return of armies from Spain, why Victor Hugo could not rest from the memory of it, and why it is so strongly woven in with the story of Charlemagne.

There is another and better reason for the quality of Carcassonne, and that is the act, to which I can recall no perfect parallel in Christian history, by which St. Louis turned what had been a living town into a mere stronghold. Every inhabitant of Carcassonne was transferred, not to suburbs, but right beyond the river, a mile and more away, to the site of that delightful town which is the Carcassonne of maps and railways, the place where the seventeenth century meets you in graceful ornaments, and where is, to my certain knowledge, the best inn south of parallel 45. St. Louis turned the rock into a mere stronghold, strengthened it, built new towers, and curtained them into that unsurpassable masonry of the central Middle Ages which you may yet admire in Aigues-Mortes and in Carnarvon.

This political act, the removal of a whole city, may have been accomplished in many other places; it is certainly recorded of many: but, for the moment at least, I can remember none except

Carcassonne in which its consequences have
remained. To this many causes have contributed,
but chiefly this, that the new town was transferred
to the open plain from the trammels of a narrow
plateau, just at the moment when all the towns of
Western Europe were growing and breaking their
bonds; just after the principal cities of North-
western Europe had got their charters, and when
Paris (the typical municipality of that age as of our
own) was trebling its area and its population.

The transference of the population once accomplished, the rock and towers of Carcassonne ceased
to change and to grow. Humanity was gone.
The fortress was still of great value in war; the
Black Prince attempted its destruction, and it is
only within living memory that it ceased to be set
down on maps (and in Government offices!) as a
fortified place: but the necessity for immediate
defence, and the labour which would have re-
modelled it, had disappeared. There had disappeared also that eager and destructive activity
which accompanies any permanent gathering of
French families. The new town on the plain
changed perpetually, and is changing still. It has
lost almost everything of the Middle Ages; it
carries, by a sort of momentum, a flavour of Louis
XIV, but the masons are at it as they are everywhere, from the Channel to the Mediterranean;
for to pull down and rebuild is the permanent

recreation of the French. The rock remains. It is put in order whenever a stone falls out of place —no one of weight has talked nonsense here against restoration, for the sense of the past is too strong—but though it is minutely and continually repaired, Old Carcassonne does not change. There is no other set of walls in Europe of which this is true.

.   .   .   .   .   .

Walking round the circuit of these walls and watching from their height the long line of the mountains, one is first held by that modern subject, the landscape, or that still more modern fascination of great hills. Next one feels what the Middle Ages designed of mass and weight and height, and wonders by what accident of the mind they so succeeded in suggesting infinity : one remembers Beauvais, which is infinitely high at evening, and the tower of Portrut, which seems bigger than any hill.

But when these commoner emotions are passed, one comes upon a very different thing. A little tower there, jutting out perilously from the wall, shows three courses of a *small red brick* set in a mortar-like stone. When I saw this kind of building I went close up and touched it with my hand. It was Roman. I knew the signal well. I had seen that brick, and picked it loose from an

Arab stable on the edge of the Sahara, and I had seen it jutting through moss on the high moors of Northumberland. I know a man who reverently brought home to Sussex such another, which he had found unbroken far beyond Damascus upon the Syrian sand.

It is easy to speak of the Empire and to say that it established its order from the Tyne to the Euphrates ; but when one has travelled alone and on foot up and down the world and seen its vastness and its complexity, and yet everywhere the unity even of bricks in their courses, then one begins to understand the name of Rome.

LYNN

EVERY man that lands in Lynn feels all through him the antiquity and the call of the town ; but especially if he comes, as I came in with another man in springtime, from the miles and miles of emptiness and miles of bending grass and the shouting of the wind. After that morning, in which one had been a little point on an immense plane, with the gale not only above one, as it commonly is, but all around one as it is at sea ; and after having steeped one's mind in the peculiar loneliness which haunts a stretch of ill-defined and wasted shore, the narrow, varied, and unordered streets of the port enhance the creations of man and emphasize his presence.

Words so few are necessarily obscure. Let me expand them. I mean that the unexpected turning of the ways in such a port is perpetually revealing something new ; that the little spaces frame, as it were, each unexpected sight : thus at the end of a street one will catch a patch of the Fens beyond the river, a great moving sail, a cloud, or the sculptured corner of an excellent house.

The same history also that permitted continual encroachment upon the public thoroughfares and that built up a gradual High Street upon the line of some cow-track leading from the fields to the ferry, the spirit that everywhere permitted the powerful or the cunning to withstand authority— that history (which is the history of all our little English towns) has endowed Lynn with an endless diversity.

It is not only that the separate things in such towns are delightful, nor only that one comes upon them suddenly, but also that these separate things are so many. They have characters as men have. There is nothing of that repetition which must accompany the love of order and the presence of strong laws. The similar insistent forms which go with a strong civilization, as they give it majesty, so they give it also gloom, and a heavy feeling of finality : these are quite lacking here in England, where the poor have for so long submitted to the domination of the rich, and the rich have dreaded and refused a central government. Everything that goes with the power of individuals has added peculiarity and meaning to all the stones of Lynn. Moreover, a quality whose absence all men now deplore was once higher in England than anywhere else, save, perhaps, in the northern Italian hills. I mean ownership, and what comes from ownership—the love of home.

You can see the past effect of ownership and individuality in Lynn as clearly as you can catch affection or menace in a human voice. The outward expression is most manifest, and to pass in and out along the lanes in front of the old houses inspires in one precisely those emotions which are aroused by a human crowd.

All the roofs of Lynn and all its pavements are worthy (as though they were living beings) of individual names.

Along the river shore, from the race of the ebb that had so nearly drowned me many years before, I watched the walls that mark the edge of the town against the Ouse, and especially that group towards which the ferry-boat was struggling against the eddy and tumble of the tide.

They were walls of every age, not high, brick of a dozen harmonious tones, with the accidents, corners, and breaches of perhaps seven hundred years. Beyond, to the left, down the river, stood the masts in the new docks that were built to preserve the trade of this difficult port. Up-river, great new works of I know not what kind stood like a bastion against the plain; and in between ran these oldest bits of Lynn, somnolescent and refreshing —permanent.

The lanes up from the Ouse when I landed I found to be of a slow and natural growth, with that slight bend to them that comes, I believe, from the

drying of fishing-nets. For it is said that courts
of this kind grew up in our sea-towns all round our
eastern and the southern coast in such a manner.
It happened thus :

The town would begin upon the highest of the
bank, for it was flatter for building, drier and
easier to defend than that part next to the water.
Down from the town to the shore the fishermen
would lay out their nets to dry. How nets look
when they are so laid, their narrowness and the
curve they take, everybody knows. Then on the
spaces between the nets shanties would be built,
or old boats turned upside down for shelter, so
that the curing of fish and the boiling of tar and
the serving and parcelling of ropes could be done
under cover. Then as the number of people
grew, the squatters' land got value, and houses
were raised (you will find many small freeholds
in such rows to this day), but the lines of the
net remained in the alley-ways between the
houses.

All this I was told once by an old man who
helped me to take my boat down Breydon. He
wore trousers of a brick-red, and the stuff of them
as thick as boards, and had on also a very thick
jersey and a cap of fur. He was shaved upon his
lips and chin, but all round the rest of his face
was a beard. He smoked a tiny pipe, quite black,
and upon matters within his own experience he

was a great liar ; but upon matters of tradition I
was willing to believe him.

Within the town, when I had gained it from
that lane which has been the ferry-lane, I suppose,
since the ferry began, age and distinction were
everywhere.

Where else, thought I, in England could you
say that nine years would make no change?
Whether, indeed, the Globe had that same wine
of the nineties I could not tell, for the hour was
not congenial to wine ; but if it has some store
of its Burgundy left from those days it must
be better still by now, for Burgundy wine takes
nine years to mature, for nine years remains in the
plenitude of its powers, and for nine years more
declines into an honourable age ; and this is also
true of claret, but in claret it goes by sevens.

.   .   .   .   .   .

The open square of the town, which one looks
at from the Globe, gives one a mingled pleasure
of reminiscence and discovery.   It breaks on one
abruptly.   It is as wide as a pasture field, and
all the houses are ample and largely founded.
Indeed, throughout this country, elbow-room—the
sense that there is space enough and to spare in
such flats and under an open sky—has filled the
minds of builders.   You may see it in all the
inland towns of the Fens ; and one found it again

here upon the further bank, upon the edge of the Fens ; for though Lynn is just off the Fens, yet it looks upon their horizon and their sky, and belongs to them in spirit.

In this large and comfortable square a very steadfast and most considerable English bank is to be discovered. It is of honest brown brick ; its architecture is of the plainest ; its appearance is such that its credit could never fail, and that the house alone by its presence could conduct a digni-fied business for ever. The rooms in it are so many and so great that the owners of such a bank (having become princes by its success) could inhabit them with a majesty worthy of their new title. But who lives above his shop since Richard-son died ? And did old Richardson ? Lord knows ! . . . . Anyhow, the bank is glorious, and it is but one of the fifty houses that I saw in Lynn.

Thus, in the same street as the Globe, was a façade of stone. If it was Georgian, it was very early Georgian, for it was relieved with ornaments of a delicate and accurate sort, and the proportions were exactly satisfying to the eye that looked on it. The stone also was of that kind (Portland stone, I think) which goes black and white with age, and which is better suited than any other to the English climate.

In another house near the church I saw a roof that might have been the roof for a town. It covered the living part and the stables, and the outhouse and the brewhouse, and the barns, and for all I know the pig-pens and the pigeons' as well. It was a benediction of a roof—a roof traditional, a roof patriarchal, a roof customary, a roof of permanence and unity, a roof that physically sheltered and spiritually sustained, a roof majestic, a roof eternal. In a word, it was a roof catholic.

And what, thought I, is paid yearly in this town for such a roof as that? I do not know; but I know of another roof at Goudhurst, in Kent, which would have cost me less than £100 a year, only I could not get it for love or money.

There is also in Lynn a Custom House not very English, but very beautiful. The faces carved upon it were so vivid that I could not but believe them to have been carved in the Netherlands, and from this Custom House looks down the pinched, unhappy face of that narrow gentleman whom the great families destroyed—James II.

There is also in Lynn what I did not know was to be seen out of Sussex—a Tudor building of chipped flints, and on it the mouldering arms of Elizabeth.

The last Gothic of this Bishop's borough which the King seized from the Church clings to chance houses in little carven masks and occasional ogives: there is everywhere a feast for whatever in the mind is curious, searching, and reverent, and over the town, as over all the failing ports of our silting eastern seaboard, hangs the air of a great past time, the influence of the Baltic and the Lowlands.

. . . . . .

For these ancient places do not change, they permit themselves to stand apart and to repose, and—by paying that price—almost alone of all things in England they preserve some historic continuity, and satisfy the memories in one's blood.

. . . . . .

So having come round to the Ouse again, and to the edge of the Fens at Lynn, I went off at random whither next it pleased me to go.

THE GUNS

I HAD slept perhaps seven hours when a lantern woke me, flashed in my face, and I wondered confusedly why there was straw in my bed; then I remembered that I was not in bed at all, but on manœuvres. I looked up and saw a sergeant with a bit of paper in his hand. He was giving out orders, and the little light he carried sparkled on the gold of his great dark-blue coat.

"You, the Englishman," he said (for that was what they called me as a nickname), "go with the gunners to-day. Where is Labbé?"

Labbé (that man by profession a cook, by inclination a marquis, and now by destiny a very good driver of guns) the day before had gone on foot. To-day he was to ride. I pointed him out where he lay still sleeping. The sergeant stirred him about with his foot, and said, "Pacte and Basilique"; and Labbé grunted. In this simple way every one knew his duty—Labbé that he had another hour's sleep and more, and that he was to take my horses: I, that I must rise and get off to the square.

149

Then the sergeant went out of the barn, cursing the straw on his spurs, and I lit a match and brushed down my clothes and ran off to the square. It was not yet two in the morning.

The gunners were drawn up in a double line, and we reserve drivers stood separate (there were only a dozen of us), and when they formed fours we were at the tail. There was a lieutenant with us and a sergeant, also two bombardiers — all mounted ; and so we went off, keeping step till we were out of the town, and then marching as we chose and thanking God for the change. For it is no easy matter for drivers to march with gunners ; their swords impede them, and though the French drivers have not the ridiculous top-boots that theatricalize other armies, yet even their simple boots are not well-suited for the road.

This custom of sending forward reserve drivers on foot, in rotation, has a fine name to it. It is called " Haut-le-pied," " High-the-foot," and must therefore be old.

A little way out of the town we had leave to sing, and we began, all together, one of those long and charming songs with which the French soldiery make-believe to forget the tedium of the road and the hardship of arms.

Now, if a man desired to answer once and for all those pedants who refuse to understand the nature of military training (both those who make a silly theatre-show of it and those who make it hideous and diabolical), there could be no better way than to let him hear the songs of soldiers. In the French service, at least, these songs are a whole expression of the barrack-room; its extreme coarseness, its steady and perpetual humour, its hatred of the hard conditions of discipline; and also these songs continually portray the distant but delightful picture of things—I mean of things rare and far off—which must lie at the back of men's minds when they have much work to do with their hands and much living in the open air and no women to pour out their wine.

Moreover, these songs have another excellent quality. They show all through that splendid unconsciousness of the soldier, that inability in him to see himself from without, or to pose as civilians always think and say he poses.

We sang that morning first, the chief and oldest of the songs. It dates from the Flemish wars of Louis XIV, and is called "Auprès de ma Blonde." Every one knows the tune. Then we sang "The Song of the Miller," and then many other songs, each longer than the last. For these songs, unlike other lyrics, have it for an object to string out as many verses as possible in order to kill the endless straight roads and the weariness.

We had need to sing. No sun rose, but the day broke over an ugly plain with hardly any trees, and that grey and wretched dawn came in with a cold and dispiriting rain unrefreshed by wind. Colson, who was a foolish little man (the son of a squire), marching by my side, wondered where and how we should be dried that day. The army was for ever producing problems for Colson, and I was often his comforter. He liked to talk to me and hear about England, and the rich people and their security, and how they never served as soldiers (from luxury), and how (what he could not understand) the poor had a bargain struck with them by the rich whereby they also need not serve. I could learn from him the meaning of many French words which I did not yet know. He had some little education ; had I asked the more ignorant men of my battery, they would only have laughed, but he had read, in common books, of the differences between nations, and could explain many things to me.

Colson, then, complaining of the rain, and wondering where he should get dried, I told him to consider not so much the happy English, but rather his poor scabbard and how he should clean it after the march, and his poor clothes, all coated with mud, and needing an hour's brushing, and his poor temper, which, if he did not take great care, would make him grow up to be an anti-militarist and a byword.

So we wrangled, and it still rained. Our songs

grew rarer, and there was at last no noise but the slush of all those feet beating the muddy road, and the occasional clank of metal as a scabbard touched some other steel, or a slung carbine struck the hilt of a bayonet. It was well on in the morning when the guns caught us up and passed us; the drivers all shrouded in their coats and bending forward in the rain; the guns coated and splashed with thick mud, and the horses also, threatened hours of grooming. I looked mine up and down as Labbé passed on them, and I groaned, for it is a rule that a man grooms his own horses whether he has ridden them or no, and after all, day in and day out, it works fair. The guns disappeared into the mist of rain, and we went on through more hours of miserable tramping, seeing no spire ahead of us, and unable to count on a long halt.

Still, as we went, I noticed that we were on some great division, between provinces perhaps, or between river valleys, for in France there are many bare upland plateaus dividing separate districts; and it is a feature of the country that the districts so divided have either formed separate provinces in the past or, at any rate (even if they have not had political recognition), have stood, and do still stand, for separate units in French society. It was more apparent with every mile as we went on that we were approaching new things. The plain was naked save for rare planted trees, and here and there, a long way off (on the horizon, it seemed) a farm or two, unprotected and alone.

The rain ceased, and the steady grey sky broke a little as we marched on, still in silence, and by this time thirsty and a little dazed. A ravine opened in a bare plateau, and we saw that it held a little village. They led us into it, down a short steep bit of road, and lined us up by a great basin of sparkling water, and every man was mad to break ranks and drink; but no one dared. The children of the village gathered in a little group and looked at us, and we envied their freedom. When we had stood thus for a quarter of an hour or so, an orderly came riding in all splashed, and his horse's coat rough with the rain and steaming up into the air. He came up to the lieutenant in command and delivered an order; then he rode away fast northward along the ravine and out of the village. The lieutenant, when he had gone, formed us into a little column, and we, who had expected to dismiss at any moment, were full of anger, and were sullen to find that by some wretched order or other we had to take another hour of the road: first we had to go back four miles along the road we had already come, and then to branch off perpendicular to our general line of march, and (as it seemed to us) quite out of our way.

It is a difficult thing to move a great mass of

men through a desolate country by small units
and leave them dependent on the country, and it
is rather wonderful that they do it so neatly and
effect the junctions so well; but the private soldier,
who stands for those little black blocks on the
military map, has a boy's impatience in him; and
a very wise man, if he wishes to keep an army in
spirit, will avoid counter-marching as much as he
can, for—I cannot tell why—nothing takes the
heart out of a man like having to plod over again
the very way he has just come. So, when we had
come to a very small village in the waste and
halted there, finding our guns and drivers already
long arrived, we made an end of a dull and meaningless day—very difficult to tell of, because the
story is merely a record of fatigue. But in a
diary of route everything must be set down faith-
fully; and so I have set down all this sodden and
empty day.

That night I sat at a peasant's table and heard
my four stable-companions understanding everything, and evidently in their world and at home,
although they were conscripts. This turned me
silent, and I sat away from the light, looking at
the fire and drying myself by its logs. As I heard
their laughter I remembered Sussex and the woods
above Arun, and I felt myself to be in exile.
Then we slept in beds, and the goodwife had our
tunics dry by morning, for she also had a son in

the service, who was a long way off at Lyons, and was not to return for two years.

.   .   .   .   .   .

There are days in a long march when a man is made to do too much, and others when he is made to do what seems meaningless, doubling backward on his road, as we had done ; there are days when he seems to advance very little; but they are not days of repose, for they are full of halting and doubts and special bits of work.   Such a day had come to us with the next dawn.

The reason of all these things—I mean, of the over-long marches, of the counter-marches, and of the short days—was the complexity of the only plan by which a great number of men and guns can be taken from one large place to another without confusion by the way—living, as they must do, upon the country, and finding at the end of every march water and hay for the horses, food and some kind of shelter for the men.   And this plan, as I have said before, consists (in a European country) in dividing your force, marching by roads more or less parallel, and converging, after some days, on the object of the march.

It is evident that in a somewhat desolate region of small and distant hamlets the front will be broader and the columns smaller, but when a large town stands in the line of march, advantage will be taken of it to mass one's men.

Such a town was Bar-le-Duc, and it was because our battery was so near to it that this fourth day was a short march of less than eight miles.

They sent the gunners in early; we drivers started later than usual, and the pace was smart at first under a happy morning sun, but still around us were the bare fields, all but treeless, and the road was part of the plain, not divided by hedges. The bombardier trotted by my side and told me of the glories of Rheims, which was his native town. He was a mild man, genial and good, and little apt for promotion. He interlarded his conversation with official remarks to show a zeal he never felt, telling one man that his traces were slack, and another that his led-horse was shirking, and after each official remark he returned up abeam of me to tell me more of the riches and splendour of Rheims. He chose me out for this favour because I already knew the countryside of the upper Champagne, and had twice seen his city. He promised me that when we got our first leave from camp he would show me many sights in the town; but this he said hoping that I would pay for the entertainment, as indeed I did.

We did not halt, nor did we pass the gunners that morning; but when we had gone about four miles or so the road began to descend through a wide gully, and we saw before us the secluded and fruitful valley of the Meuse. It is here of an even width for miles, bounded by regular low hills. We were coming down the eastern wall of that valley, and on the parallel western side a similar height, with similar ravines and gullies leading down to the river, bounded our narrow view.   I caught the distant sound of trumpets up there beyond us, and nearer was the unmistakable rumble of the guns.   The clatter of horses below in the valley road and the shouting of commands were the signs that the regiment was meeting. The road turned.   On a kind of platform, just before it joined the main highway, a few feet above it, we halted to wait our order—and we saw the guns go by !

Only half the regiment was to halt at Bar-le-Duc. But six batteries, thirty-six guns, their men, horses, apparatus, forges, and waggons occupying and advancing in streams over a valley are a wonderful sight.   Clouds of dust and the noise of metal woke the silent places of the Meuse, and sometimes river birds would rise and wheel in the air as the clamour neared them.   Far off a lonely battery was coming down the western slope to join the throng in its order, and for some reason their two trumpets were still playing the march and lending to this great display the unity of music. We dismounted and watched from the turf of the roadside a pageant which the accident of an ordered and servile life afforded us; for it is true of armies that the compensation of their drudgery and miserable subjection is the continual opportunity of these large emotions; and not only by their vastness and arrangement, but by the very fact that they merge us into themselves, do armies widen the spirit of a man and give it communion with the majesty of great numbers.   One becomes a part of many men.

The seventh battery, with which we had little to do (for in quarters they belonged to the furthest corner from our own), first came by and passed us, with that interminable repetition of similar things which is the note of a force on the march, and makes it seem like a river flowing.   We recognized it by the figure of one Chevalier, a major attached to them.   He was an absent-minded man of whom many stories were told—kindly, with a round face; and he wore eye-glasses, either for the distinction they afforded or because he was short of sight.   The seventh passed us, and their forge and waggon ended the long train.   A regulation space between them and the next allowed the dust to lie a little, and then the ninth came by; we knew them well, because in quarters they were our neighbours.   At their head was their captain, whose name was Levy.   He was a Jew, small, very sharp-featured, and a man who worked astonishingly hard.   He was very popular with his men, and his battery was happy and boasted.

He cared especially for their food, and would go
into their kitchen daily to taste the soup.   He was
also a silent man.   He sat his horse badly, bent
and crouched, but his eyes were very keen; and he
again was a character of whom the men talked and
told stories.   I believe he was something of a
mathematician; but we knew little of such things
where our superiors were concerned.

As the ninth battery passed us we were given
the order to mount, and knew that our place came
next.   The long-drawn *Ha-a-lte!* and the lifted
swords down the road contained for a while the
batteries that were to follow, and we filed out of
our side road into the long gap they had left us.
Then, taking up the trot ourselves, we heard the
order passing down infinitely till it was lost in
the length of the road; the trumpets galloped
past us and formed at the head of the column; a
much more triumphant noise of brass than we had
yet heard heralded us with a kind of insolence,
and the whole train with its two miles and more of
noisy power gloried into the old town of Bar-le-
Duc, to the great joy of its young men and
women at the windows, to the annoyance of the
householders, to the stupefaction of the old, and
doubtless to the ultimate advantage of the Republic.

When we had formed park in the grey market-
square, ridden our horses off to water at the

river and to their quarters, cleaned kit and harness, and at last were free—that is, when it was already evening—Matthieu, a friend of mine who had come by another road with his battery, met me strolling on the bridge. Matthieu was of my kind, he had such a lineage as I had and such an education. We were glad to meet. He told me of his last halting-place—Pagny—hidden on the upper river. It is the place where the house of Luxembourg are buried, and some also of the great men who fell when Henry V of England was fighting in the North, and when on this flank the Eastern dukes were waging the Burgundian wars. It was not the first time that the tumult of men in arms had made echoes along the valley.

Matthieu and I went off together to dine. He lent me a pin of his, a pin with a worked head, to pin my tunic with where it was torn, and he begged me to give it back to him. But I have it still, for I have never seen him since ; nor shall I see him, nor he me, till the Great Day.

THE LOOE STREAM

OF the complexity of the sea, and of how it is manifold, and of how it mixes up with a man, and may broaden or perfect him, it would be very tempting to write; but if one once began on this, one would be immeshed and drowned in the metaphysic, which never yet did good to man nor beast. For no one can eat or drink the metaphysic, or take any sustenance out of it, and it has no movement or colour, and it does not give one joy or sorrow; one cannot paint it or hear it, and it is too thin to swim about in. Leaving, then, all these general things, though they haunt me and tempt me, at least I can deal little by little and picture by picture with that sea which is perpetually in my mind, and let those who will draw what philosophies they choose. And the first thing I would like to describe is that of a place called the Looe Stream, through which in a boat only the other day I sailed for the first time, noticing many things.

When St. Wilfrid went through those bare heaths and coppices, which were called the forest

of Anderida, and which lay all along under the
Surrey Downs, and through which there was a
long, deserted Roman road, and on this road a
number of little brutish farms and settlements (for
this was twelve hundred years ago), he came out
into the open under the South Downs, and crossed
my hills and came to the sea plain, and there he
found a kind of Englishman more savage than the
rest, though Heaven knows they were none of them
particularly refined or gay.   From these Englishmen the noble people of Sussex are descended.

Already the rest of England had been Christian
a hundred years when St. Wilfrid came down into
the sea plain, and found, to his astonishment, this
sparse and ignorant tribe.   They were living in
the ruins of the Roman palaces ; they were too
stupid to be able to use any one of the Roman
things they had destroyed.   They had kept, perhaps, some few of the Roman women, certainly all
the Roman slaves.   They had, therefore, vague
memories of how the Romans tilled the land.

But those memories were getting worse and
worse, for it was nearly two hundred years since
the ships of Aella had sailed into Shoreham (which
showed him to be a man of immense determination,
for it is a most difficult harbour, and there were
then no piers and lights)—it was nearly two hundred
years, and there was only the least little glimmering
twilight left of the old day.   These barbarians

were going utterly to pieces, as barbarians ever will when they are cut off from the life and splendour of the South. They had become so cretinous and idiotic, that when St. Wilfrid came wandering among them they did not know how to get food. There was a famine, and as their miserable religion, such as it was (probably it was very like these little twopenny-halfpenny modern heresies of their cousins, the German pessimists) —their religion, I say, not giving them the jolly energy which all decent Western religion gives a man, they being also by the wrath of God deprived of the use of wine (though tuns upon tuns of it were waiting for them over the sea a little way off, but probably they thought their horizon was the end of the world)—their religion, I say, being of this nature, they had determined, under the pressure of that famine which drove them so hard, to put an end to themselves, and St. Wilfrid saw them tying themselves together in bands (which shows that they knew at least how to make rope) and jumping off the cliffs into the sea. This practice he determined to oppose.

He went to their king—who lived in Chichester, I suppose, or possibly at Bramber—and asked him why the people were going on in this fashion, who said to him : " It is because of the famine."

St. Wilfrid, shrugging his shoulders, said: "Why do they not eat fish?"

" Because," said the King, " fish, swimming
about in the water, are almost impossible to catch.
We have tried it in our hunger a hundred times,
but even when we had the good luck to grasp one
of them, the slippery thing would glide from our
fingers."

St. Wilfrid then in some contempt said again :
" Why do you not make nets? "

And he explained the use of nets to the whole
Court, preaching, as it were, a sermon upon nets
to them, and craftily introducing St. Peter and
that great net which they hang outside his tomb in
Rome upon his feast day—which is the 29th of
June. The King and his Court made a net and
threw it into the sea, and brought out a great mass
of fish. They were so pleased that they told St.
Wilfrid they would do anything he asked. He
baptized them and they made him their first bishop ;
and he took up his residence in Selsey, and since
then the people of Sussex have gone steadily forward, increasing in every good thing, until they
are now by far the first and most noble of all the
people in the world.

There is I know not what in history, or in the
way in which it is taught, which makes people
imagine that it is something separate from the life
they are living, and because of this modern error,
you may very well be wondering what on earth
this true story of the foundation of our country has

to do with the Looe Stream. It has everything to do with it. The sea, being governed by a pagan god, made war at once, and began eating up all those fields which had specially been consecrated to the Church, civilization, common sense, and human happiness. It is still doing so, and I know an old man who can remember a forty-acre field all along by Clymping having been eaten up by the sea; and out along past Rustington there is, about a quarter of a mile from the shore, a rock, called the Church Rock, the remains of a church which quite a little time ago people used for all the ordinary purposes of a church.

The sea then began to eat up Selsey. Before the Conquest—though I cannot remember exactly when — the whole town had gone, and they had to remove the cathedral to Chichester. In Henry VIII's time there was still a park left out of the old estates, a park with trees in it ; but this also the sea has eaten up ; and here it is that I come to the Looe Stream. The Looe Stream is a little dell that used to run through that park, and which to-day, right out at sea, furnishes the only gate by which ships can pass through the great maze of banks and rocks which go right out to sea from Selsey Bill, miles and miles, and are called the Owers.

On the chart that district is still called "The Park," and at very low tides stumps of the old trees can be seen ; and for myself I believe, though I don't think it can be proved, that in among the masses of sand and shingle which go together to make the confused dangers of the Owers you would find the walls of Roman palaces, and heads of bronze and marble, and fragments of mosaic and coins of gold.

The tide coming up from the Channel finds, rising straight out of the bottom of the sea, the shelf of this old land, and it has no avenue by which to pour through save this Looe Stream, which therefore bubbles and runs like a mill-race, though it is in the middle of the sea.

If you did not know what was underneath you, you could not understand why this river should run separate from the sea all round, but when you have noticed the depths on the chart, you see a kind of picture in your mind : the wall of that old mass of land standing feet above the floor of the Channel, and the top of what was once its fields and its villas, and its great church almost awash at low tides, and through it a cleft, which was, I say, a dell in the old park, but is now that Looe Stream buoyed upon either side, and making a river by itself running in the sea.

Sailing over it, and remembering all these things at evening, I got out of the boil and tumble into deep water. It got darker, and the light on the *Nab* ship showed clearly a long way off, and purple against the west stood the solemn height of the island. I set a course for this light, being alone at the tiller, while my two companions slept down below. When the night was full the little variable air freshened into a breeze from the south-east; it grew stronger and stronger, and lifted little hearty following seas, and blowing on my quarter drove me quickly to the west, whither I was bound. The night was very warm and very silent, although little patches of foam murmured perpetually, and though the wind could be heard lightly in the weather shrouds.

The star Jupiter shone brightly just above my wake, and over Selsey Bill, through a flat band of mist, the red moon rose slowly, enormous.

RONCESVALLES

SITTING one day in Pampeluna, which occupies the plain just below the southern and Spanish escarpment of the Pyrenees, I and another remembered with an equal desire that we had all our lives desired to see Roncesvalles and the place where Roland died. This town (we said) was that which Charlemagne destroyed upon his march to the Pass, and I, for my part, desired here, as in every other part of Europe where I had been able to find his footsteps, to follow them, and so to re-create his time.

The road leads slantwise through the upper valleys of Navarre, crossing by passes the various spurs of the mountains, but each pass higher than the last and less frequented, for each is nearer the main range. As you leave Pampeluna the road grows more and more deserted, and the country through which it cuts more wild. The advantages of wealth which are conferred by the neighbourhood of the capital of Navarre are rapidly lost as one proceeds ; the houses grow rarer, the shrines more ruinous and more aged, until one comes at last upon the bleak valley which introduces the final approach to Roncesvalles.

The wealth and order everywhere associated with the Basque blood have wholly disappeared. This people is not receding—it holds its own, as it deserves to do ; but as there are new fields which it has occupied within the present century upon the more western hills, so there are others to the east, and this valley among them, from whence it has disappeared. The Basque names remain, but the people are no longer of the Basque type, and the tongue is forgotten.

So gradual is the ascent and so continual the little cols which have to be surmounted, that a man does not notice how much upward he is being led towards the crest of the ridge. And when he comes at last upon the grove from which he sees the plateau of Roncesvalles spread before him, he wonders that the chain of the Pyrenees (which here lie out along in cliffs like sharp sunward walls, stretching in a strict perspective to the distant horizon) should seem so low. The reason that this white wall of cliffs seems so low is that the traveller is standing upon the last of a series of great steps which have led him up towards the frontier, much as the prairies lead one up towards the Rockies in Colorado. When he has passed through the very pleasant wood which lies directly beneath the cliffs, and reaches the little village of Roncesvalles itself, he wonders still more that so famous a pass should be so small a thing. The pass from this side is so broad, with so low a saddle of grass, that it seems more like the crossing of the Sussex Downs than the crossing of an awful range of mountains. It is a rounded gap, up to which there lifts a pretty little wooded combe; and no one could be certain, during the half-hour spent in climbing such a petty summit, that he was, in so climbing, conquering Los Altos, the high Pyrenees.

But when the summit is reached, then the meaning of the "*Imus Pyrenæus*," and the place that passage has taken in history, is comprehended in a moment. One sees at what a height one was in that plain of Roncesvalles, and one sees how the main range dominates the world; for down below one an enormous cleft into the stuff of the mountains falls suddenly and almost sheer, and you see unexpectedly beneath you the approach from France into Spain. The gulf at its narrowest is tremendous; but, more than that, when the floor of the valley is reached, that floor itself slopes away down and down by runs and by cascades towards the very distant plains of the north, upon which the funnel debouches. Moreover, it was up this gulf, and from the north, that the armies came; it was this vision of a precipice that seized them when their leaders had determined to invade the Peninsula. This also was what, for so many generations, so many wanderers must have seen who came to wonder at the place where the rear-guard of Charlemagne had been destroyed.

The whole of the slope is covered with an ancient wood, and this wood is so steep that it would be impossible or dangerous to venture down it. The old Carolingian road skirts the mountain-side with difficulty, clinging well up upon its flank; the great modern road, which is excellent and made for artillery, has to go even nearer the summit; below them there falls away a slant or edge to which the huge beech trees cling almost parallel to the steep earth, running their perpendicular lines so high and close against the hill that they look like pines. As you peer down in among the trunks, you see the darkness increasing until the eye can penetrate no more, and dead, enormous trees that have lived their centuries, and have fallen perhaps for decades, lie across the aisles of the wood, propped up against their living fellows; for, by one of those political accidents which are common throughout the whole length of the Pyrenees, both sides of the watershed belong to Spain, so that no Government or modern energy has come to disturb the silence. One would swear that the last to order this wood were the Romans.

I had thought to find so famous a valley peopled, or at least visited. I found it utterly alone, and even free from travellers, as though the wealthier part of Europe had forgotten the most famous of Christian epics. I saw no motor-cars, nor any women—only at last, in the very depths of the valley, a boy cutting grass in a tiny patch of open land. And it was hereabouts, so far as I could make out, that the Peers were killed.

The song, of course, makes them fall on the far side of the summit, upon the fields of Roncesvalles, with the sun setting right at them along the hills. And that is as it should be, for it is evident that (in a poem) the hero fighting among hills should die upon the enemy's side of the hills. But that is not the place where Roland really died. The place where he really died, he and Oliver and Turpin and all the others, was here in the very recess of the Northern Valley. It was here only that rocks could have been rolled down upon an army, and here is that narrow, strangling gorge where the line of march could most easily have been cut in two by the fury of the mountaineers. Also Eginhard says very clearly that they had already passed the hills and seen France, and that is final. It was from these cliffs, then, that such an echo was made by the horn of Roland, and it was down that funnel of a valley that the noise grew until it filled Christendom ; and it was up that gorge that there came, as it says in the song—

> The host in a tide returning :
> Charles the King and his Barony.

This was the place.   And any man who may yet
believe (I know such a discussion is pedantry)—
any man who may yet believe the song of Roland
to have been a Northern legend had better come to
this place and drink the mountains in.   For whoever wrote—

> High are the hills and huge and dim with cloud,
> Down in the deeps, the living streams are loud,

had certainly himself stood in the silence and
majesty of this valley.

It was already nearly dark when we two men
had clambered down to that place, and up between
the walls of the valley we had already seen the
early stars.   We pushed on to the French frontier
in an eager appetite for cleanliness and human
food.

The last Spanish town is called Val Carlos, as it
ought to be, considering that Charlemagne himself had once come roaring by.   When we reached
it in the darkness we had completed a forced
march of forty-two miles, going light, it is true,
and carrying nothing each of us but a gourd of
wine and a sack, but we were very tired.   There,
at the goal of our effort, one faint sign of government and of men at last appeared.   It was in
character with all the rest.   One might not cross
the frontier upon the road without a written leave.
The written leave was given us, and in half an
hour Spain was free.

THE SLANT OFF THE LAND

WE live a very little time. Before we have reached the middle of our time perhaps, but not long before, we discover the magnitude of our inheritance. Consider England. How many men, I should like to know, have discovered before thirty what treasures they may work in her air? She magnifies us inwards and outwards; her fields can lead the mind down towards the subtle beginning of things; the tiny iridescence of insects; the play of light upon the facets of a blade of grass. Her skies can lead the mind up infinitely into regions where it seems to expand and fill, no matter what immensities.

It was the wind off the land that made me think of all this possession in which I am to enjoy so short a usufruct. I sat in my boat holding that tiller of mine, which is not over firm, and is but a rough bar of iron. There was no breeze in the air, and the little deep vessel swung slightly to the breathing of the sea. Her great mainsail and her balloon-jib came over lazily as she swung, and filled themselves with the cheating semblance of a wind. The boom creaked in the goose-neck, and at every roll the slack of the mainsheet tautened with a kind of little thud which thrilled the deck behind me. I saw under the curve of my head-sail the long and hazy line, which is the only frontier of England; the plain that rather marries with than defies her peculiar seas. For it was in the Channel, and not ten miles from the coast-line of my own county, that these thoughts rose in me during the calm at the end of winter, and the boat was drifting down more swiftly than I knew upon the ebb of the outer tide. Far off to the south sunlight played upon the water, and was gone again. The great ships did not pass near me, and so I sat under a hazy sky restraining the slight vibration of the helm and waiting for the wind.

In whatever place a man may be the spring will come to him. I have heard of men in prison who would note the day when its influence passed through the narrow window that was their only communion with their kind. It comes even to men in cities; men of the stupid political sort, who think in maps and whose interest is in the addition of numbers. Indeed, I have heard such men in London itself expressing pleasure when a south-west gale came up in April from over the pines of Hampshire and of Surrey and mixed the Atlantic with the air of the fields. To me this year the spring came suddenly, like a voice speaking, though a low one—the voice of a person subtle, remembered, little-known, and always desired. For a wind blew off the land.

The surface of the sea northward between me and the coast of Sussex had been for so many hours elastic, smooth, and dull, that I had come to forget the indications of a change. But here and there, a long way off, little lines began to show, which were indeed broad spaces of ruffled water, seen edgeways from the low free-board of my boat. These joined and made a surface all the way out towards me, but a surface not yet revealed for what it was, nor showing the movement and life and grace of waves. For no light shone upon it, and it was not yet near enough to be distinguished. It grew rapidly, but the haze and silence had put me into so dreamy a state that I had forgotten the ordinary anxiety and irritation of a calm, nor had I at the moment that eager expectancy of movement which should accompany the sight of that dark line upon the sea.

Other things possessed me, the memory of home and of the Downs. There went before this breeze, as it were, attendant servants, outriders who brought with them the scent of those first flowers in the North Wood or beyond Gumber Corner, and the fragrance of our grass, the savour which the sheep know at least, however much the visitors to my dear home ignore it.   A deeper sympathy even than that of the senses came with those messengers and brought me the beeches and the yew trees also, although I was so far out at sea, for the loneliness of this great water recalled the loneliness of the woods, and both those solitudes—the real and the imaginary —mixed in my mind together as they might in the mind of a sleeping man.

Before this wind as it approached, the sky also cleared : not of clouds, for there were none, but of that impalpable and warm mist which seems to us, who know the south country and the Channel, to be so often part of the sky, and to shroud without obscuring the empty distances of our seas.   There was a hard clear light to the north ; and even over the Downs, low as they were upon the horizon, there was a sharp belt of blue.   I saw the sun strike the white walls of Lady Newburgh's Folly, and I saw, what had hitherto been all confused, the long line of the Arundel Woods contrasting with the plain.   Then the boom went over to port, the jib filled, I felt the helm pulling steadily for the first time in so many hours, and the boat responded.   The wind was on me ; and though it was from the north, that wind was warm, for it came from the sheltered hills.

Then, indeed, I quite forgot those first few moments, which had so little to do with the art of sailing, and which were perhaps unworthy of the full life that goes with the governing of sails and rudders. For one thing, I was no longer alone ; a man is never alone with the wind—and the boat made three. There was work to be done in pressing against the tiller and in bringing her up to meet the seas, small though they were, for my boat was also small. Life came into everything ; the Channel leapt and (because the wind was across the tide) the little waves broke in small white tips: in their movement and my own, in the dance of the boat and the noise of the shrouds, in the curtsy of the long sprit that caught the ridges of foam and lifted them in spray, even in the free streaming of that loose untidy end of line which played in the air from the leech, as young things play from wantonness, in the rush of the water, just up to and sometimes through the lee scuppers, and in the humming tautness of the sheet, in everything about me there was exuberance and joy. The sun upon the twenty million faces of the waves made music rather than laughter, and the energy which this first warmth of the year had spread all over the Channel and shore, while it made life one, seemed also to make it innumerable. We were now not only three, the wind and my boat and I : we were all part (and masters for the moment) of a great throng. I knew them all by their names, which I had learnt a long time ago, and had sung of

them in the North Sea. I have often written them
down. I will not be ashamed to repeat them here,
for good things never grow old. There was the
Wave that brings good tidings, and the Wave
that breaks on the shore, and the Wave of the
island, and the Wave that helps, and the Wave
that lifts forrard, the kindly Wave and the youngest
Wave, and Amathea the Wave with bright hair, all
the waves that come up round Thetis in her train
when she rises from the side of the old man, her
father, where he sits on his throne in the depth of
the sea ; when she comes up cleaving the water
and appears to her sons in the upper world.

The Wight showed clear before me. I was
certain with the tide of making the Horse Buoy and
Spithead while it was yet afternoon, and before the
plenitude of that light and movement should have
left me. I settled down to so much and such
exalted delight as to a settled task. I lit my pipe
for a further companion (since it was good to add
even to so many). I kept my right shoulder only
against the tiller, for the pressure was now steady
and sound. I felt the wind grow heavy and
equable, and I caught over my shoulder the merry
wake of this very honest moving home of mine as
she breasted and hissed through the sea.

Here, then, was the proper end of a long cruise.
It was spring time, and the season for work on
land. I had been told so by the heartening wind.

And as I went still westward, remembering the duties of the land, the sails still held full, the sheets and the weather shrouds still stood taut and straining, and the little clatter of the broken water spoke along the lee rail.   And so the ship sailed on.

'Εν δ' ἄνεμος πρῆσεν μέσον ἰσίον, ἀμφὶ δὲ κῦμα
Στείρῃ πορφύρεον μεγάλ' ἴαχε, νηὸς ἰούσης.

THE CANIGOU

A MAN might discuss with himself what it was that made certain great sights of the world famous, and what it is that keeps others hidden. This would be especially interesting in the case of mountains. For there is no doubt that there is a modern attraction in mountains which may not endure, but which is almost as intense in our generation as it was in that of our fathers. The emotion produced by great height and by the something unique and inspiring which distinguishes a mountain from a hill has bitten deeply into the modern mind. Yet there are some of the most astounding visions of this sort in Europe which are, and will probably remain, unemphasized for travellers.

The vision of the Bernese Oberland when it breaks upon one from the crest of Jura has been impressed—upon English people, at least—in two fine passages: the one written by Ruskin, the other, if I remember right, in a book called *A Cruise upon Wheels*. The French have, I believe, no classical presentment of that view, nor perhaps have the Germans. The line of the Alps as one sees it upon very clear days from the last of the Apennines—this, I think, has never been properly praised in any modern book—not even an Italian. The great red mountain-face which St. Bruno called "the desert" I do not remember to have read of anywhere nor to have heard described; for it stands above an unfrequented valley, and the regular approach to the Chartreuse is from the other side. Yet it is something which remains as vivid to those few who have suddenly caught sight of it from a turn of the Old Lyons road as though they had seen it in a fantastic dream. That astonishing circle of cliffs which surrounds Bourg d'Oisans, though it has been written of now and then, has not, so to speak, taken root in people's imagination.

Even in this country there are twenty great effects which, though they have, of course, suffered record, are still secure from general praise; for instance, that awful trench which opens under your feet, as it were, up north and beyond Plynlimmon. It is a valley as unexpected and as incredible in its steepness and complete isolation as any one may see in the drawings of the romantic generation of English water-colour, yet perhaps no one has drawn it; there is certainly no familiar picture of it anywhere.

When one comes to think of it, the reason of

such exceptions to fame as are these is usually that such and such an unknown but great sight lies off the few general roads of travel. It is a vulgar reason, but the true one. Unless men go to a mountain to climb because it is difficult to climb, or unless it often appears before them along one of their main journeys, it will remain quiet. Among such masses is the Canigou.

Here is a mountain which may be compared to Etna. It is lower, indeed, in the proportion of nine to eleven ; but when great isolated heights of this sort are in question, such a difference hardly counts. It can be seen, as Etna can, from the sea, though it stands a good deal more inland ; it dominates, as Etna does, a very famous plain, but modern travel does nothing to bring it into the general consciousness of the world. If Spain were wealthy, or if the Spanish harbours naturally led to any place which all the rich desired to visit, the name of the Canigou would begin to grow. Where the railway skirts the sea from Narbonne to Barcelona, it is your permanent companion for a good hour in the express, and for any time you like in the ordinary trains. During at least three months in the year, its isolation is peculiarly relieved and marked by the snow, which lies above an even line all along its vast bulk. It is also one of those mountains in which one can recognize the curious regularity of the " belts " which text-books talk of. There are great forests at the base of it, just above the hot Mediterranean plain ; the beech comes higher than the olive, the pines last of all ; after them the pastures and the rocks. In the end of February a man climbs up from a spring that is as southern as Africa to a winter that is as northern as the highlands of Scotland, and all the while he feels that he is climbing nothing confused or vague, but one individual peak which is the genius of the whole countryside.

This countryside is the Roussillon, a lordship as united as the Cerdagne ; it speaks one language, shows one type of face, and is approached by but a small group of roads, and each road passes through a mountain gap. For centuries it went with Barcelona. It needed the Revolution to make it French, and it is full of Spanish memories to this day.

For the Roussillon depends upon the Canigou just as the Bay of Syracuse depends upon Etna, or that of Naples upon Vesuvius, and its familiar presence has sunk into the patriotism of the Roussillon people, as those more famous mountains have into the art and legends of their neighbours. There are I know not how many monographs upon the Canigou, but not one has been translated, I would wager, into any foreign language.

Yet it is the mountain which very many men who have hardly heard its name have been looking for all their lives. It gives as good camping as is to be had in the whole of the Pyrenees. I believe there is fishing, and perhaps one can shoot. Properly speaking, there is no climbing in it ; at least, one can walk up it all the way if one chooses the right path, but there is everything else men look for when they escape from cities. It is so big that you would never learn it in any number of camps, and the change of its impressions is perpetual. From the summit the view has two interests—of colour and of the past. You have below you a plain like an inlaid work of chosen stones : the whole field is an arrangement of different culture and of bright rocks and sand ; and below you, also, in a curve, is all that coast which at the close of the Roman Empire was, per- haps, the wealthiest in Europe. In the extreme north a man might make out upon a clear day the bulk of Narbonne. Perpignan is close by ; the little rock harbour of Venus, Port Vendres, is to the south. From the plain below one, which has always been crammed with riches, sprang the chief influences of Southern Gaul. It was here that the family of Charlemagne took its origin, and it was perhaps from here that he saw, through the windows of a palace, that fleet of pirates which moved him to his sad prophecy. That plain, moreover, will re-arise ; it is still rich, and all the Catalan province of Spain below it, of which it is the highway and the approach, must increase in value before Europe from year to year. The vast development of the French African territory is re-acting upon that coast : all it needs is a central harbour, and if that harbour were formed it would do what Narbo did for the Romans at the end of their occupation—it would tap, much better than does Cette, the wealth of Gascony, perhaps, also, an Atlantic trade, and its exchanges towards Africa and the Levant. The Mediterranean, which is perpetually increasing in wealth and in importance to-day, would have a second Marseilles, and should such a port arise—then, when our ships and our travellers are familiar with it, the Canigou (if it cares for that sort of thing) will be as happy as the Matterhorn. For the present it is all alone.

THE MAN AND HIS WOOD

I KNEW a man once that was a territorial mag-
nate and had an estate in the county of Berkshire. I will not conceal his name. It was William
Frederick Charles Hermann-Postlethwaite.

On his estate was a large family mansion, surrounded by tasteful gardens of a charming old
kind, and next outside these a great park, well
timbered. But the thing I am going to talk
about was a certain wood of which he was rightly
very proud. It stood on the slope of a grass
down, just above the valley, and beneath it was
a clean white road, and a little way along that
a town, part of which belonged to Mr. Hermann-
Postlethwaite, part to a local solicitor and money-
lender, several bits to a brewer in Reading, and a
few houses to the inhabitants. The people in the
town were also fond of the wood, and called it
"The Old Wood." It was not very large, but, as
I have said before, it was very beautiful, and contained all manner of trees, but especially beeches,
under which nothing will grow—as the poet puts
it in Sussex :   Unner t' beech and t' yow
                 Nowt 'll grow.

Well, as years passed, Mr. Hermann-Postle-thwaite became fonder and fonder of the wood. He began towards 1885 to think it the nicest thing on his estate—which it was; and he would often ride out to look at it of a morning on his grey mare "Betsy." When he rode out like this of a morning his mount was well groomed, and so was he, however early it might be, and he would carry a little cane to hit the mare with and also as a symbol of authority. The people who met him would touch their foreheads, and he would wave his hand genially in reply. He was a good fellow. But the principal thing about him was his care for the old wood; and when he rode out to look at it, as I say, he would speak to any one around so early—his bailiff, as might be, or sometimes his agent, or even the foreman of the workshop or the carpenter, or any hedger or ditcher that might be there, and point out bits of the wood, and say, "That branch looks pretty dicky. No harm to cut that off short and parcel and serve the end and cap it with a zinc cap"; or, "Better be cutting the Yartle Bush for the next fallow, it chokes the gammon-rings, and I don't like to see so much standard ivy about, it's the death of trees." I am not sure that I have got the technical words right, but at any rate they were more or less like that, for I have heard him myself time and again. I often used to go out with him on another horse, called Sultan, which he lent me to ride upon.

Well, he got fonder and fonder of this wood, and kept on asking people what he should do, and how one could make most use of it, and he worried a good deal about it. He read books about woods, and in the opening of 1891 he had down to stay with him for a few days a man called Churt, who had made a great success with woods on the Warra-Warra. But Churt was a vulgar fellow, and so Hermann - Postlethwaite's wife, Lady Gwynnys Hermann-Postlethwaite, would not have him in the house again, which was a bother. Her husband then rode over to see another man, and the upshot of it was that he put up a great board saying "Trespassers in this wood will be prosecuted," and it might as well not have been put up, for no one ever went into the wood, not even from the little town, because it was too far for them to walk, and, anyhow, they did not care for walking. And as for the doctor's son, a boy of thirteen, who went in there with an air-gun to shoot things, he paid no attention to the board.

The next thing my friend did was to have a fine strong paling put all round the wood in March, 1894. This paling was of oak; it was seven feet high; it had iron spikes along the top. There were six gates in it, and stout posts at intervals of ten yards. The boards overlapped very exactly.

It was as good a bit of work as ever I saw. He had it varnished, and it looked splendid. All this took two years.

Just then he was elected to Parliament, not for Berkshire, as you might have imagined, but for a slum division of Birmingham. He was very proud of this, and quite rightly too. He said: " I am the only Conservative member in the Midlands." It almost made him forget about his wood. He shut up the Berkshire place and took a house in town, and as he could not afford Mayfair, and did not understand such things very well, the house he took was an enormous empty house in Bayswater, and he had no peace until he gave it up for a set of rooms off Piccadilly ; and then his mother thought that looked so odd that he did the right thing, and got into a nice old-fashioned furnished house in Westminster, overlooking the Green Park.

But all this cost him a mint of money, and politics made him angrier and angrier. They never let him speak, and they made him vote for things he thought perfectly detestable. Then he did speak, and as he was an honest English gentleman the papers called him ridiculous names and said he had no brains. So he just jolly well threw the whole thing up and went back to Berkshire, and everybody welcomed him, and he did a thing he had never done before : he put a flag up

over his house to show he was at home.   Then he
began to think of his wood again.

The very first time he rode out to look at it he
found the paling had given way in places from
the fall of trees, and that some leaned inwards
and some outwards, and that one of the gates was
off its hinges.   There were also two cows walking
about in the wood, and what annoyed him most of
all, the iron spikes were rusty and the varnish had
all gone rotten and white and streaky on the
palings.   He spoke to the bailiff about this, and
hauled him out to look at it.   The bailiff rubbed
the varnish with his finger, smelt it, and said that
it had perished.   He also said that there was no
such thing as good varnish nowadays, and he
added that there wasn't any varnish, not the very
best, but wouldn't go like that with rain and all.
Mr. Hermann-Postlethwaite grumbled a good
deal, but he supposed the bailiff knew best ; so he
told him to see what could be done, and for several
weeks he heard no more about it.

I forgot to tell you that about this time the
South African War had broken out, and as things
were getting pretty tangled, Hermann-Postlethwaite went out with his regiment, the eighth
battalion, not of the Berkshire, but of the Orkney
regiment.   While he was out there, his brother,
in Dr. Charlbury's home, died, and he succeeded
to the baronetcy.   As he already had a V.C. and

was now given a D.S.O., as well as being one of
the people mentioned in dispatches, he was pretty
important by the time he came home, when the
war was over, just before the elections of 1900.

When he got home he had a splendid welcome,
both from his tenants in Berkshire in passing
through and from those of his late brother in the
big place in Worcestershire. He preferred his
Berkshire place, however, and, letting the big
place to an American of the name of Hendrik K.
Boulge, he went back to his first home. When
he got there he thought of the old wood, and went
out to look at it. The palings were mended, but
they were covered all over with tar ! He was ex-
ceedingly angry, and ordered them to be painted
at once ; but the bailiff assured him one could
not paint over tar, and so did the carpenter and
the foreman. At this he had a fit of rage, and
ordered the whole damned thing to be pulled
down, and swore he would be damned if he ever
had a damned stick or a rail round the damned
wood again. He was no longer young ; he was
getting stout and rather puffy; he was not so
reasonable as of old. Anyhow, he had the whole
thing pulled down. Next year (that is, in 1901) his
wife died.

I wish I had the space to tell you all the other
things he did to the wood. How a friend of his
having sold a similar wood on the Thames in

building lots at £500 an acre, he put up the old wood at the same rate.   How, the old wood being 200 acres in extent, he hoped to make £100,000 out of it.   How he thought this a tidy sum.   How he got no offers at this price, nor at £100, nor at £50.   How an artist offered him £20 for half an acre to put up a red tin bungalow upon.   How he lost his temper with the artist.   How at last he left the whole thing alone and tried to forget all about it. .

.   .   .   .   .   .

The old wood to-day is just like what it was when I wandered in it as a boy.   The doctor's son is a man now, and is keeping a bar in Sydney ; so he is gone.   The townspeople don't come any more than before.   I am the only person who goes near the place.   The trees are a trifle grander.   I happen now and then, when I visit this Berkshire parish, upon a stump of a post or an old spike in the grass of this wood, but otherwise it is as though all this had not been.

A solemn thought : How enduring are the works of Nature—how perishable those of Man !

THE CHANNEL

FRIENDS of mine, friends all, and you also, publishers, colonials and critics, do you know that particular experience for which I am trying to find words? Do you know that glamour in the mind which arises and transforms our thought when we see the things that the men who made us saw—the things of a long time ago, the origins? I think everybody knows that glamour, but very few people know where to find it.

Every man knows that he has in him the power for such revelations, and every man wonders in what strange place he may come upon them. There are men also (very rich) who have considered all the world and wandered over it, seeking those first experiences and trying to feel as felt the earlier men in a happier time—yet these few rich men have not so felt and have not so found the things which they desire. I have known men who have thought to find them in the mountains, but would not climb them simply enough and refused to leave their luxuries behind, and so lost everything, and might as well have been walking in a dirty town at home for all the little good that the mountains did to them.   And I know men who have thought to find this memory and desire in foreign countries, in Africa, hunting great beasts such as our fathers hunted; yet even these have not relit those old embers, which if they lie dead and dark in a man make his whole soul dusty and useless, but which if they be once rekindled can make him part of all the centuries.

Yet there is a simple and an easy way to find what the men who made us found, and to see the world as they saw it, and to take a bath, as it were, in the freshness of beginnings; and that is to go to work as cheaply and as hardly as you can, and only as much away from men as they were away from men, and not to read or to write or to think, but to eat and drink and use the body in many immediate ways, which are at the feet of every man. Every man who will walk for some days carelessly, sleeping rough when he must, or in poor inns, and making for some one place direct because he desires to see it, will know the thing I mean.   And there is a better way still of which I shall now speak: I mean, to try the seas in a little boat not more than twenty-five feet long, preferably decked, of shallow draught, such as can enter into all creeks and havens, and so simply rigged that by oneself, or with a friend at most, one can wander all over the world.

Certainly every man that goes to sea in a little boat of this kind learns terror and salvation, happy living, air, danger, exultation, glory and repose at the end; and they are not words to him, but, on the contrary, realities which will afterwards throughout his life give the mere words a full meaning. And for this experiment there lies at our feet, I say, the Channel.

It is the most marvellous sea in the world—the most suited for these little adventures; it is crammed with strange towns, differing one from the other; it has two opposite people upon either side, and hills and varying climates, and the hundred shapes and colours of the earth, here rocks, there sand, there cliffs, and there marshy shores. It is a little world. And what is more, it is a kind of inland sea.

People will not understand how narrow it is, crossing it hurriedly in great steamships; nor will they make it a home for pleasure unless they are rich and can have great boats; yet they should, for on its water lies the best stage for playing out the old drama by which the soul of a healthy man is kept alive. For instance, listen to this story :—

The sea being calm, and the wind hot, uncertain, and light from the east, leaving oily gaps on the water, and continually dying down, I drifted one morning in the strong ebb to the South Goodwin Lightship, wondering what to do. There was

a haze over the land and over the sea, and through
the haze great ships a long way off showed, one
or two of them, like oblong targets which one fires
at with guns.   They hardly moved in spite of all
their canvas set, there was so little breeze.   So
I drifted in the slow ebb past the South Goodwin,
and I thought: "What is all this drifting and
doing nothing?   Let us play the fool, and see if
there are no adventures left."

So I put my little boat about until the wind took
her from forward, such as it was, and she crawled
out to sea.

It was a dull, uneasy morning, hot and silent,
and the wind, I say, was hardly a wind, and most
of the time the sails flapped uselessly.

But after eleven o'clock the wind first rose, and
then shifted a little, and then blew light but steady;
and then at last she heeled and the water spoke
under her bows, and still she heeled and ran, until
in the haze I could see no more land; but ever so
far out there were no seas, for the light full breeze
was with the tide, the tide ebbing out as a strong,
and silent as a man in anger, down the hidden
parallel valleys of the narrow sea.   And I held this
little wind till about two o'clock, when I drank wine
and ate bread and meat at the tiller, for I had
them by me, and just afterwards, still through a
thick haze of heat, I saw Griz-nez, a huge ghost,
right up against and above me; and I wondered,

for I had crossed the Channel, now for the first time, and knew now what it felt like to see new land.

Though I knew nothing of the place, I had this much sense, that I said to myself: "The tide is right down Channel, racing through the hidden valleys under the narrow sea, so it will all go down together and all come up together, and the flood will come on this foreign side much at the same hour that it does on the home side." My boat lay to the east and the ebb tide held her down, and I lit a pipe and looked at the French hills and thought about them and the people in them, and England which I had left behind, and I was delighted with the loneliness of the sea; and still I waited for the flood.

But in a little while the chain made a rattling noise, and she lay quite slack and swung oddly; and then there were little boiling and eddying places in the water, and the water seemed to come up from underneath sometimes, and altogether it behaved very strangely, and this was the turn of the tide. Then the wind dropped also, and for a moment she lollopped about, till at last, after I had gone below and straightened things, I came on deck to see that she had turned completely round, and that the tide at last was making up my way, towards Calais, and her chain was taut and her nose pointed down Channel, and a little westerly breeze, a little draught of air, came up cool along the tide.

When this came I was very glad, for I saw that I could end my adventure before night. So I pulled up the anchor and fished it, and then turned with the tide under me, and the slight half-felt breeze just barely filling the mainsail (the sheet was slack, so powerless was the wind), and I ran up along that high coast, watching eagerly every new thing ; but I kept some way out for fear of shoals, till after three good hours under the reclining sun of afternoon, which glorified the mist, I saw, far off, the roofs and spires of a town, and a low pier running well out to sea, and I knew that it must be Calais. And I ran for these piers, careless of how I went, for it was already half of the spring flood tide, and everything was surely well covered for so small a boat, and I ran up the fairway in between the piers, and saw Frenchmen walking about and a great gun peeping up over its earth-work, and plenty of clean new masonry. And a man came along and showed me where I could lie ; but I was so strange to the place that I would not take a berth, but lay that night moored to an English ship.

And when I had eaten and drunk and everything was stowed away and darkness had fallen, I went on deck, and for a long time sat silent, smoking a pipe and watching the enormous lighthouse of

Calais, which is built right in the town, and which turns round and round above one all night long.

And I thought: "Here is a wonderful thing! I have crossed the Channel in this little boat, and I know now what the sea means that separates France from England. I have strained my eyes for shore through a haze. I have seen new lands, and I feel as men do who have dreamt dreams."

But in reality I had had very great luck indeed, and had had no right to cross, for my coming back was to be far more difficult and dreadful, and I was to suffer many things before again I could see tall England, close by me, out of the sea.

But how I came back, and of the storm, and of its majesty, and of how the boat and I survived, I will tell you another time, only imploring you to do the same; not to tell of it, I mean, but to sail it in a little boat.

THE MOWING OF A FIELD

THERE is a valley in South England remote
from ambition and from fear, where the
passage of strangers is rare and unperceived, and
where the scent of the grass in summer is breathed
only by those who are native to that unvisited land.
The roads to the Channel do not traverse it; they
choose upon either side easier passes over the
range. One track alone leads up through it to the
hills, and this is changeable: now green where
men have little occasion to go, now a good road
where it nears the homesteads and the barns. The
woods grow steep above the slopes; they reach
sometimes the very summit of the heights, or,
when they cannot attain them, fill in and clothe the
combes. And, in between, along the floor of the
valley, deep pastures and their silence are bordered
by lawns of chalky grass and the small yew trees
of the Downs.

The clouds that visit its sky reveal themselves
beyond the one great rise, and sail, white and
enormous, to the other, and sink beyond that
other. But the plains above which they have

travelled and the Weald to which they go, the people of the valley cannot see and hardly recall. The wind, when it reaches such fields, is no longer a gale from the salt, but fruitful and soft, an inland breeze ; and those whose blood was nourished here feel in that wind the fruitfulness of our orchards and all the life that all things draw from the air.

In this place, when I was a boy, I pushed through a fringe of beeches that made a complete screen between me and the world, and I came to a glade called No Man's Land. I climbed beyond it, and I was surprised and glad, because from the ridge of that glade I saw the sea. To this place very lately I returned.

The many things that I recovered as I came up the countryside were not less charming than when a distant memory had enshrined them, but much more. Whatever veil is thrown by a longing recollection had not intensified nor even made more mysterious the beauty of that happy ground; not in my very dreams of morning had I, in exile, seen it more beloved or more rare. Much also that I had forgotten now returned to me as I approached —a group of elms, a little turn of the parson's wall, a small paddock beyond the graveyard close, cherished by one man, with a low wall of very old stone guarding it all around. And all these things fulfilled and amplified my delight, till even the good vision of the place, which I had kept so many years, left me and was replaced by its better reality. "Here," I said to myself, "is a symbol of what some say is reserved for the soul: pleasure of a kind which cannot be imagined save in the moment when at last it is attained."

When I came to my own gate and my own field, and had before me the house I knew, I looked around a little (though it was already evening), and I saw that the grass was standing as it should stand when it is ready for the scythe. For in this, as in everything that a man can do—of those things at least which are very old— there is an exact moment when they are done best. And it has been remarked of whatever rules us that it works blunderingly, seeing that the good things given to man are not given at the precise moment when they would have filled him with delight. But, whether this be true or false, we can choose the just turn of the seasons in every- thing we do of our own will, and especially in the making of hay. Many think that hay is best made when the grass is thickest; and so they delay until it is rank and in flower, and has already heavily pulled the ground. And there is another false reason for delay, which is wet weather. For very few will understand (though it comes year after year) that we have rain always in South England between the sickle and the scythe, or say just after the weeks of east wind are over. First we have a week of sudden warmth, as though the South had come to see us all ; then we have the weeks of east and south-east wind ; and then we have more or less of that rain of which I spoke, and which always astonishes the world.   Now it is just before, or during, or at the very end of that rain—but not later—that grass should be cut for hay.   True, upland grass, which is always thin, should be cut earlier than the grass in the bottoms and along the water meadows ; but not even the latest, even in the wettest seasons, should be left (as it is) to flower and even to seed.   For what we get when we store our grass is not a harvest of something ripe, but a thing just caught in its prime before maturity : as witness that our corn and straw are best yellow, but our hay is best green.   So also Death should be represented with a scythe and Time with a sickle ; for Time can take only what is ripe, but Death comes always too soon.   In a word, then, it is always much easier to cut grass too late than too early ; and I, under that evening and come back to these pleasant fields, looked at the grass and knew that it was time.   June was in full advance : it was the beginning of that season when the night has already lost her foothold of the earth and hovers over it, never quite descending, but mixing sunset with the dawn.

Next morning, before it was yet broad day, I awoke, and thought of the mowing.   The birds were already chattering in the trees beside my window, all except the nightingale, which had left and flown away to the Weald, where he sings all summer by day as well as by night in the oaks and the hazel spinneys, and especially along the little river Adur, one of the rivers of the Weald. The birds and the thought of the mowing had awakened me, and I went down the stairs and along the stone floors to where I could find a scythe ; and when I took it from its nail, I remembered how, fourteen years ago, I had last gone out with my scythe, just so, into the fields at morning. In between that day and this were many things, cities and armies, and a confusion of books, mountains and the desert, and horrible great breadths of sea.

When I got out into the long grass the sun was not yet risen, but there were already many colours in the eastern sky, and I made haste to sharpen my scythe, so that I might get to the cutting before the dew should dry. Some say that it is best to wait till all the dew has risen, so as to get the grass quite dry from the very first. But, though it is an advantage to get the grass quite dry, yet it is not worth while to wait till the dew has risen. For, in the first place, you lose many hours of work (and those the coolest), and next— which is more important—you lose that great ease and thickness in cutting which comes of the dew. So I at once began to sharpen my scythe.

There is an art also in the sharpening of a scythe, and it is worth describing carefully. Your blade must be dry, and that is why you will see men rubbing the scythe-blade with grass before they whet it. Then also your rubber must be quite dry, and on this account it is a good thing to lay it on your coat and keep it there during all your day's mowing. The scythe you stand upright, with the blade pointing away from you, and you put your left hand firmly on the back of the blade, grasping it: then you pass the rubber first down one side of the blade-edge and then down the other, beginning near the handle and going on to the point and working quickly and hard. When you first do this you will, perhaps, cut your hand; but it is only at first that such an accident will happen to you.

To tell when the scythe is sharp enough this is the rule. First the stone clangs and grinds against the iron harshly; then it rings musically to one note; then, at last, it purrs as though the iron and stone were exactly suited. When you hear this, your scythe is sharp enough; and I, when I heard it in that June dawn, with everything quite silent except the birds, let down the scythe and bent myself to mow.

When one does anything anew, after so many years, one fears very much for one's trick or habit. But all things once learnt are easily recoverable, and I very soon recovered the swing and power of the mower. Mowing well and mowing badly—or rather not mowing at all—are separated by very little ; as is also true of writing verse, of playing the fiddle, and of dozens of other things, but of nothing more than of believing. For the bad or young or untaught mower without tradition, the mower Promethean, the mower original and contemptuous of the past, does all these things : He leaves great crescents of grass uncut. He digs the point of the scythe hard into the ground with a jerk. He loosens the handles and even the fastening of the blade. He twists the blade with his blunders, he blunts the blade, he chips it, dulls it, or breaks it clean off at the tip. If any one is standing by he cuts him in the ankle. He sweeps up into the air wildly, with nothing to resist his stroke. He drags up earth with the grass, which is like making the meadow bleed. But the good mower who does things just as they should be done and have been for a hundred thousand years, falls into none of these fooleries. He goes forward very steadily, his scythe-blade just barely missing the ground, every grass falling ; the swish and rhythm of his mowing are always the same.

So great an art can only be learnt by continual practice ; but this much is worth writing down, that, as in all good work, to know the thing with

which you work is the core of the affair. Good
verse is best written on good paper with an easy
pen, not with a lump of coal on a whitewashed
wall. The pen thinks for you ; and so does the
scythe mow for you if you treat it honourably and
in a manner that makes it recognize its service.
The manner is this. You must regard the scythe
as a pendulum that swings, not as a knife that
cuts. A good mower puts no more strength into
his stroke than into his lifting. Again, stand up
to your work. The bad mower, eager and full of
pain, leans forward and tries to force the scythe
through the grass. The good mower, serene and
able, stands as nearly straight as the shape of the
scythe will let him, and follows up every stroke
closely, moving his left foot forward. Then also
let every stroke get well away. Mowing is a thing
of ample gestures, like drawing a cartoon. Then,
again, get yourself into a mechanical and repeti-
tive mood : be thinking of anything at all but
your mowing, and be anxious only when there
seems some interruption to the monotony of the
sound. In this mowing should be like one's
prayers—all of a sort and always the same, and so
made that you can establish a monotony and work
them, as it were, with half your mind : that happier half, the half that does not bother.

In this way, when I had recovered the art after
so many years, I went forward over the field, cut-

ting lane after lane through the grass, and bringing out its most secret essences with the sweep of
the scythe until the air was full of odours.   At the
end of every lane I sharpened my scythe and
looked back at the work done, and then carried
my scythe down again upon my shoulder to begin
another.   So, long before the bell rang in the
chapel above me—that is, long before six o'clock,
which is the time for the *Angelus*—I had many
swathes already lying in order parallel like soldiery ; and the high grass yet standing, making
a great contrast with the shaven part, looked dense
and high.   As it says in the *Ballad of Val-ès-
Dunes*, where—

> The tall son of the Seven Winds
> Came riding out of Hither-hythe,

and his horse-hoofs (you will remember) trampled
into the press and made a gap in it, and his sword
(as you know)

> . . . was like a scythe
> In Arcus when the grass is high
> And all the swathes in order lie,
> And there's the bailiff standing by
> A-gathering of the tithe.

So I mowed all that morning, till the houses
awoke in the valley, and from some of them rose a
little fragrant smoke, and men began to be seen.

I stood still and rested on my scythe to watch
the awakening of the village, when I saw coming

up to my field a man whom I had known in older
times, before I had left the Valley.

He was of that dark silent race upon which all
the learned quarrel, but which, by whatever meaningless name it may be called—Iberian, or Celtic,
or what you will—is the permanent root of all
England, and makes England wealthy and preserves it everywhere, except perhaps in the Fens
and in a part of Yorkshire. Everywhere else you
will find it active and strong. These people are
intensive; their thoughts and their labours turn
inward. It is on account of their presence in these
islands that our gardens are the richest in the
world. They also love low rooms and ample fires
and great warm slopes of thatch. They have, as I
believe, an older acquaintance with the English
air than any other of all the strains that make up
England. They hunted in the Weald with stones,
and camped in the pines of the green-sand. They
lurked under the oaks of the upper rivers, and saw
the legionaries go up, up the straight paved road
from the sea. They helped the few pirates to
destroy the towns, and mixed with those pirates
and shared the spoils of the Roman villas, and
were glad to see the captains and the priests
destroyed. They remain; and no admixture of
the Frisian pirates, or the Breton, or the Angevin
and Norman conquerors, has very much affected
their cunning eyes.

To this race, I say, belonged the man who now approached me. And he said to me, "Mowing?" And I answered, "Ar." Then he also said "Ar," as in duty bound; for so we speak to each other in the Stenes of the Downs.

Next he told me that, as he had nothing to do, he would lend me a hand; and I thanked him warmly, or, as we say, "kindly." For it is a good custom of ours always to treat bargaining as though it were a courteous pastime; and though what he was after was money, and what I wanted was his labour at the least pay, yet we both played the comedy that we were free men, the one granting a grace and the other accepting it. For the dry bones of commerce, avarice and method and need, are odious to the Valley; and we cover them up with a pretty body of fiction and observances. Thus, when it comes to buying pigs, the buyer does not begin to decry the pig and the vendor to praise it, as is the custom with lesser men; but tradition makes them do business in this fashion :—

First the buyer will go up to the seller when he sees him in his own steading, and, looking at the pig with admiration, the buyer will say that rain may or may not fall, or that we shall have snow or thunder, according to the time of year. Then the seller, looking critically at the pig, will agree that the weather is as his friend maintains. There

is no haste at all ; great leisure marks the dignity
of their exchange. And the next step is, that the
buyer says : "That's a fine pig you have there,
Mr. ——" (giving the seller's name). "Ar, powerful fine pig." Then the seller, saying also " Mr."
(for twin brothers rocked in one cradle give each
other ceremonious observance here), the seller,
I say, admits, as though with reluctance, the
strength and beauty of the pig, and falls into deep
thought. Then the buyer says, as though moved
by a great desire, that he is ready to give so much
for the pig, naming half the proper price, or a
little less. Then the seller remains in silence for
some moments ; and at last begins to shake his
head slowly, till he says : "I don't be thinking
of selling the pig, anyways." He will also add
that a party only Wednesday offered him so
much for the pig—and he names about double the
proper price. Thus all ritual is duly accomplished ; and the solemn act is entered upon with
reverence and in a spirit of truth. For when the
buyer uses this phrase : "I'll tell you what I *will*
do," and offers within half a crown of the pig's
value, the seller replies that he can refuse him
nothing, and names half a crown above its value ;
the difference is split, the pig is sold, and in the
quiet soul of each runs the peace of something
accomplished.

Thus do we buy a pig or land or labour or malt

or lime, always with elaboration and set forms; and many a London man has paid double and more for his violence and his greedy haste and very unchivalrous higgling. As happened with the land at Underwaltham, which the mortgagees had begged and implored the estate to take at twelve hundred, and had privately offered to all the world at a thousand, but which a sharp direct man, of the kind that makes great fortunes, a man in a motor-car, a man in a fur coat, a man of few words, bought for two thousand three hundred before my very eyes, protesting that they might take his offer or leave it; and all because he did not begin by praising the land.

Well then, this man I spoke of offered to help me, and he went to get his scythe. But I went into the house and brought out a gallon jar of small ale for him and for me; for the sun was now very warm, and small ale goes well with mowing. When we had drunk some of this ale in mugs called "I see you," we took each a swathe, he a little behind me because he was the better mower; and so for many hours we swung, one before the other, mowing and mowing at the tall grass of the field. And the sun rose to noon and we were still at our mowing; and we ate food, but only for a little while, and we took again to our mowing. And at last there was nothing left but a small square of grass, standing like a square of

linesmen who keep their formation, tall and unbroken, with all the dead lying around them when
a battle is over and done.

Then for some little time I rested after all those
hours; and the man and I talked together, and
a long way off we heard in another field the
musical sharpening of a scythe.

The sunlight slanted powdered and mellow over
the breadth of the valley; for day was nearing its
end. I went to fetch rakes from the steading;
and when I had come back the last of the grass
had fallen, and all the field lay flat and smooth,
with the very green short grass in lanes between
the dead and yellow swathes.

These swathes we raked into cocks to keep them
from the dew against our return at daybreak; and
we made the cocks as tall and steep as we could,
for in that shape they best keep off the dew, and
it is easier also to spread them after the sun has
risen. Then we raked up every straggling blade,
till the whole field was a clean floor for the tedding
and the carrying of the hay next morning. The
grass we had mown was but a little over two
acres; for that is all the pasture on my little tiny
farm.

When we had done all this, there fell upon us
the beneficent and deliberate evening; so that as
we sat a little while together near the rakes, we
saw the valley more solemn and dim around us,

and all the trees and hedgerows quite still, and held by a complete silence.   Then I paid my companion his wage, and bade him a good night, till we should meet in the same place before sunrise.

He went off with a slow and steady progress, as all our peasants do, making their walking a part of the easy but continual labour of their lives. But I sat on, watching the light creep around towards the north and change, and the waning moon coming up as though by stealth behind the woods of No Man's Land.

THE ROMAN ROAD

THE other day (it was Wednesday, and the air was very pure) I went into the stable upon my way towards the wood, and there I saw my horse Monster standing by himself, regarding nothingness.   And when I had considered what a shame it was to take one's pleasure in a wood and leave one's helpless horse at home, I bridled him and saddled him and took him out, and rode him the way that I had meant to go alone.   So we went together along the Stene under the North Wood until we got to the edge of the forest, and then we took the green Ride to the right, for it was my intention to go and look at the Roman road.

Behind my house, behind my little farm, there are as many miles of turf as one cares to count, and then behind it also, but the other way, there goes this deep and lonely forest.   It is principally of beech, which is the tree of the chalk, and no one has cut it or fenced it or thought about it (except to love it), since the parts about my village took their names: Gumber and Fairmile

Bay Combe, the Nore, and the stretch called No Man's Land.

Into the darkness of these trees I rode very quietly with Monster, my horse, but whether the autumn air were pleasanter to him or to me neither of us could decide, for there is no bridge between two souls.   That is, if horses have a soul, which I suppose they have, for they are both stupid and kindly, and they fear death as though a part, and but a part, of them were immortal.   Also they see things in the dark and are cognizant of evil.

When I had gone some hundred yards towards the Roman road I saw, bending lower than the rest on the tree from which it hung, a golden bough, and I said to myself that I had had good luck, for such a thing has always been the sign of an unusual experience and of a voyage among the dead.   All the other leaves of the tree were green, but the turn of the year, which sends out foragers just as the spring does, marking the way it is to go, had come and touched this bough and changed it, so that it shone out by itself in the recesses of the forest and gleamed before and behind.   I did not ask what way it led me, for I knew ; and so I went onwards, riding my horse, until I came to that long bank of earth which runs like a sort of challenge through this ancient land to prove what our origins were, and who first brought us merry people into the circuit of the world.

When I saw the Roman road the sharper influence which it had had upon my boyhood returned to me, and I got off my horse and took his bit out of his mouth so that he could play the fool with the grass and leaves (which are bad for him), and I hitched the snaffle to a little broken peg of bough so that he could not wander. And then I looked up and down along the boles of the great North Wood, taking in the straight line of the way.

I have heard it said that certain professors, the most learned of their day, did once deny that this was a Roman road. I can well believe it, and it is delightful to believe that they did. For this road startles and controls a true man, presenting an eternal example of what Rome could do. The peasants around have always called it the "Street." It leads from what was certainly one Roman town to what was certainly another. That sign of Roman occupation, the modern word "Cold Harbour," is scattered up and down it. There are Roman pavements on it. It goes plumb straight for miles, and at times, wherever it crosses undisturbed land, it is three or four feet above the level of the down. Here, then, was a feast for the learned: since certainly the more obvious a thing is, the more glory there must be in denying it. And deny it they did (or at least, so I am told) just as they will deny that Thomas à Becket was a Papist, or that

Austerlitz was fought in spite of Trafalgar, or that the Gospel of St. John is the Gospel of St. John.

Here, then, sitting upon this Roman road I considered the nature of such men, and when I had thought out carefully where the nearest Don might be at that moment, I decided that he was at least twenty-three miles away, and I was very glad : for it permitted me to contemplate the road with common sense and with Faith, which is Common Sense transfigured; and I could see the Legionaries climbing the hill. I remembered also what a sight there was upon the down above, and I got upon my horse again to go and see it.

When one has pushed one's way through the brambles and the rounded great roots which have grown upon this street—where no man has walked perhaps for about a thousand years—one gets to the place where it tops the hill, and here one sees the way in which the line of it was first struck out. From where one stands, right away like a beam, leading from rise to rise, it runs to the cathedral town. You see the spot where it enters the eastern gate of the Roman walls; you see at the end of it, like the dot upon an "i," the mass of the cathedral. Then, if you turn and look northward, you see from point to point its taut stretch across the weald to where, at the very limit of the horizon, there is a gap in the chain of hills that bars your view.

The strict design of such a thing weighs upon one as might weigh upon one four great lines of Virgil, or the sight of those enormous stones which one comes upon, Roman also, in the Algerian sands. The plan of such an avenue by which to lead great armies and along which to drive commands argues a mixture of unity and of power as intimate as the lime and the sand of which these conquerors welded their imperishable cement. And it does more than this. It suggests swiftness and certitude of aim and a sort of eager determination which we are slow to connect with Government, but which certainly underlay the triumph of this people. A road will give one less trouble if it winds about and feels the contours of the land. It will pay better if it is of earth and broken stones instead of being paved, nor would any one aiming at wealth or comfort alone laboriously raise its level, as the level of this road is raised. But in all that the Romans did there was something of a monument. Where they might have taken pipes down a valley and up the opposing side they preferred the broad shoulders of an arcade, and where a seven-foot door would have done well enough to enter their houses by they were content with nothing less than an arch of fifty. In all their work they were conscious of some business other than that immediately to hand, and therefore it is possible that their ruins will survive the establishment of our own time as they have survived that of the Middle Ages.   In this wild place, at least, nothing remained of all that was done between their time and ours.

These things did the sight on either side of the summit suggest to me, but chiefly there returned as I gazed the delicious thought that learned men, laborious and heavily endowed, had denied the *existence* of this Roman road.

See with what manifold uses every accident of human life is crammed !   Here was a piece of pedantry and scepticism, which might make some men weep and some men stamp with irritation, and some men, from sheer boredom, fall asleep, but which fed in my own spirit a fountain of pure joy, as I considered carefully what kind of man it is who denies these things ; the kind of way he walks ; the kind of face he has; the kind of book he writes; the kind of publisher who chisels him; and the kind of way in which his works are bound.   With every moment my elation grew greater and more impetuous, until at last I could not bear to sit any longer still, even upon so admirable a beast, nor to look down even at so rich a plain (though that was seen through the air of Southern England), but turning over the downs I galloped home, and came in straight from the turf to my own ground—for what man would live upon a high road who could go through a gate right off the turf to his own steading and let the world go hang ?

And so did I. But as they brought me beer and bacon at evening, and I toasted the memory of things past, I said to myself : " Oxford, Cambridge, Dublin, Durham—you four great universities—you terrors of Europe—that road is older than you : and meanwhile I drink to your continued healths, but let us have a little room . . . air, there, give us air, good people. I stifle when I think of you."

THE ONION-EATER

THERE is a hill not far from my home whence it is possible to see northward and southward such a stretch of land as is not to be seen from any eminence among those I know in Western Europe. Southward the sea-plain and the sea standing up in a belt of light against the sky, and northward all the weald.

From this summit the eye is disturbed by no great cities of the modern sort, but a dozen at least of those small market towns which are the delight of South England hold the view from point to point, from the pale blue downs of the island over, eastward, to the Kentish hills.

A very long way off, and near the sea-line, the high faint spire of that cathedral which was once the mother of all my county goes up without weight into the air and gathers round it the delicate and distant outlines of the landscape—as, indeed, its builders meant that it should do. In such a spot, on such a high watch-tower of England, I met, three days ago, a man.

I had been riding my kind and honourable horse

for two hours, broken, indeed, by a long rest in a deserted barn.

I had been his companion, I say, for two hours, and had told him a hundred interesting things—to which he had answered nothing at all—when I took him along a path that neither of us yet had trod. I had not, I know; he had not (I think), for he went snorting and doubtfully. This path broke up from the kennels near Waltham, and made for the High Wood between Gumber and No Man's Land. It went over dead leaves and quite lonely to the thick of the forest; there it died out into a vaguer and a vaguer trail. At last it ceased altogether, and for half an hour or so I pushed carefully, always climbing upwards, through the branches, and picked my way along the bramble-shoots, until at last I came out upon that open space of which I have spoken, and which I have known since my childhood. As I came out of the wood the south-west wind met me, full of the Atlantic, and it seemed to me to blow from Paradise.

I remembered, as I halted and so gazed north and south to the weald below me, and then again to the sea, the story of that Sultan who publicly proclaimed that he had possessed all power on earth, and had numbered on a tablet with his own hand each of his happy days, and had found them, when he came to die, to be seventeen. I knew what that heathen had meant, and I looked into my heart as

I remembered the story, but I came back from the examination satisfied, for "So far," I said to myself, "this day is among my number, and the light is falling. I will count it for one." It was then that I saw before me, going easily and slowly across the downs, the figure of a man.

He was powerful, full of health and easy; his clothes were rags; his face was open and bronzed. I came at once off my horse to speak with him, and, holding my horse by the bridle, I led it forward till we met. Then I asked him whither he was going, and whether, as I knew these open hills by heart, I could not help him on his way.

He answered me that he was in no need of help, for he was bound nowhere, but that he had come up off the high road on to the hills in order to get his pleasure and also to see what there was on the other side. He said to me also, with evident enjoyment (and in the accent of a lettered man), "This is indeed a day to be alive!"

I saw that I had here some chance of an adventure, since it is not every day that one meets upon a lonely down a man of culture, in rags and happy. I therefore took the bridle right off my horse and let him nibble, and I sat down on the bank of the Roman road holding the leather of the bridle in my hand, and wiping the bit with plucked grass. The stranger sat down beside me, and drew from his pocket a piece of bread and a large onion. We then talked of those things which should chiefly occupy mankind : I mean, of happiness and of the destiny of the soul. Upon these matters I found him to be exact, thoughtful, and just.

First, then, I said to him : "I also have been full of gladness all this day, and, what is more, as I came up the hill from Waltham I was inspired to verse, and wrote it inside my mind, completing a passage I had been working at for two years, upon joy. But it was easy for me to be happy, since I was on a horse and warm and well fed ; yet even for me such days are capricious. I have known but few in my life. They are each of them distinct and clear, so rare are they, and (what is more) so different are they in their very quality from all other days."

"You are right," he said, "in this last phrase of yours. . . . They are indeed quite other from all the common days of our lives. But you were wrong, I think, in saying that your horse and clothes and good feeding and the rest had to do with these curious intervals of content. Wealth makes the run of our days somewhat more easy, poverty makes them more hard—or very hard. But no poverty has ever yet brought of itself despair into the soul—the men who kill themselves are neither rich nor poor. Still less has wealth ever purchased those peculiar hours. I also am filled with their spirit to-day, and God knows," said he, cutting his onion in two, so that it gave out a strong savour, "God knows I can purchase nothing."

"Then tell me," I said, "whence do you believe these moments come? And will you give me half your onion?"

"With pleasure," he replied, "for no man can eat a whole onion; and as for that other matter, why, I think the door of heaven is ajar from time to time, and that light shines out upon us for a moment between its opening and closing." He said this in a merry, sober manner; his black eyes sparkled, and his large beard was blown about a little by the wind. Then he added: "If a man is a slave to the rich in the great cities (the most miserable of mankind), yet these days come to him. To the vicious wealthy and privileged men, whose faces are stamped hard with degradation, these days come; they come to you, you say, working (I suppose) in anxiety like most of men. They come to me who neither work nor am anxious so long as South England may freely import onions."

"I believe you are right," I said. "And I especially commend you for eating onions; they contain all health; they induce sleep; they may be called the apples of content, or, again, the companion-fruits of mankind."

"I have always said," he answered gravely,

"that when the couple of them left Eden they hid and took away with them an onion.   I am moved in my soul to have known a man who reveres and loves them in the due measure, for such men are rare."

Then he asked, with evident anxiety : " Is there no inn about here where a man like me will be taken in ? "

" Yes," I told him.   " Down under the Combe at Duncton is a very good inn.   Have you money to pay ?   Will you take some of my money ? "

" I will take all you can possibly afford me," he answered in a cheerful, manly fashion.   I counted out my money and found I had on me but 3s. 7d. " Here is 3s. 7d.," I said.

" Thank you, indeed," he answered, taking the coins and wrapping them in a little rag (for he had no pockets, but only holes).

" I wish," I said with regret, " we might meet and talk more often of many things.   So much do we agree, and men like you and me are often lonely."

He shrugged his shoulders and put his head on one side, quizzing at me with his eyes.   Then he shook his head decidedly, and said : " No, no—it is certain that we shall never meet again."   And thanking me with great fervour, but briefly, he went largely and strongly down the escarpment of the Combe to Duncton and the weald ; and I shall never see him again till the Great Day. . . .

THE RETURN TO ENGLAND

I N Calais harbour, it being still very early in the morning, about half-past five, I peered out to see how things were looking, for if that coast corresponded at all to ours, the tide should be making westerly by six o'clock that day—the ebb tide—and it was on the first of that tide that I should make the passage to England, for at sea you never can tell. At sea you never can tell, and you must take every inch the gods allow you. You will need that and more very often before evening. Now, as I put my head out I saw that I could not yet start, for there was a thick white mist over everything, so that I could not even see the bowsprit of my own boat. Everything was damp : the decks smelt of fog, and from the shore came sounds whose cause I could not see. Looking over the iron bulwarks of the big English cargo ship, alongside of which I was moored, was a man with his head upon his folded arms. He told me that he thought the fog would lift ; and so I waited, seeking no more sleep, but sitting up there in the drifting fog, and taking pleasure in a bugle call which the French call "La Diane," and which they play to wake the soldiers. But in summer it wakes nobody, for all the world is waking long before.

Towards six the mist blew clean away before a little air from the north-east; it had come sharp over those miles and miles of sand dunes and flats which stretch away from Gris-nez on to Denmark. From Gris-nez all the way to the Sound there is no other hill; but coarse grass, wind-swept and flying sand. Finding this wind, I very quickly set sail, and as I did not know the harbour I let down the peak of the mainsail, that she might sail slowly, and crept along close to the eastern pier, for fear that when I got to the open work the westerly tide should drive me against the western pier; but there was no need for all this caution, since the tide was not yet making strongly. Yet was I wise to beware, for if you give the strange gods of the sea one little chance they will take a hundred, and drown you for their pleasure. And sailing, if you sail in all weathers, is a perpetual game of skill against them, the heartiest and most hazardous game in the world.

So then, when I had got well outside, I found what is called "a lump." The sea was jumbling up and down irregularly, as though great animals had just stopped fighting there. But whatever was the cause of it, this lump made it difficult to

manage the boat I was in, for the air was still light
and somewhat unsteady ; sometimes within a point
of north, and then again dropping and rising free
within a point of east : on the whole, north-east.
To windward the sea was very clear, but down
towards the land there was a haze, and when I got
to that black buoy which is three miles from
Calais, and marks the place where you should turn
to go into the harbour, I could barely see the high
land glooming through the weather, and Calais
belfry and lighthouse tower I could not see at
all.   I looked at my watch and saw it was seven,
and immediately afterwards the wind became
steady and true, and somewhat stronger, and the
work began.

She would point very nearly north, and so I laid
her for that course, though that would have taken
me right outside the Goodwins, for I knew that
the tide was making westerly down the Channel,
ebbing away faster and faster, and that, like a man
crossing a rapid river in a ferry-boat, I had to
point up far above where I wanted to land, which
was at Dover, the nearest harbour.   I sailed her,
therefore, I say, as close as she would lie, and the
wind rose.

The wind rose, and for half an hour I kept her
to it.   She had no more sail than she needed ; she
heeled beautifully and strongly to the wind ; she
took the seas, as they ran more regular, with a

motion of mastery. It was like the gesture of a horse when he bends his head back to his chest, arching his neck with pride as he springs upon our Downs at morning. So set had the surging of the sea become that she rose and fell to it with rhythm, and the helm could be kept quite steady, and the regular splash of the rising bows and the little wisps of foam came in ceaseless exactitude like the marching of men, and in all this one mixed with the life of the sea.

But before it was eight o'clock (and I had eaten nothing) the wind got stronger still, and I was anxious and gazed continuously into it, up to windward, seeing the white caps beginning on the tops of the seas, although the wind and tide were together. She heeled also much more, and my anxiety hardened with the wind, for the wind had strengthened by about half past eight, so that it was very strong indeed, and she was plainly over-canvased, her lee rail under all the time and all the cordage humming ; there it stood, and by the grace and mercy of God the wind increased no more, for its caprice might have been very different.

Then began that excellent game which it is so hard to play, but so good to remember, and in which all men, whether they admit it or not, are full of fear, but it is a fear so steeped in exhilaration that one would think the personal spirit of the sea was mingled with the noise of the air.

For a whole great hour she roared and lifted through it still, taking the larger seas grandly, with disdain, as she had taken the smaller, and still over the buried lee rail the stream of the sea went by rejoicing and pouring, and the sheets and the weather runner trembled with the vigour of the charge, and on she went, and on. I was weary of the seas ahead (for each and individually they struck my soul as they came, even more strongly than they struck the bows—steep, curling, unintermittent, rank upon rank upon rank, an innumerable cavalry); still watching them, I say, I groped round with my hand behind the cabin door and pulled out brandy and bread, and drank brandy and ate bread, still watching the seas. And, as men are proud of their companions in danger, so I was proud to see the admirable lift and swing of that good boat, and to note how, if she slowed for a moment under the pounding, she recovered with a stride, rejoicing; and as for my fears, which were now fixed and considerable, I found this argument against them: that, though I could see nothing round me but the sea, yet soon I should be under the lee of the Goodwins, for, though I could not exactly calculate my speed, and though in the haze beyond nothing appeared, it was certain that I was roaring very quickly towards the further shore.

When, later, the sea grew confused and full of

swirls and boiling, I said to myself: "This must be the tail of the Goodwins." But it was not. For, though I did not know it, the ebb of the great spring tide had carried me right away down Channel, and there was not twelve feet of water under the keel, for the seething of the sea that I noticed came from the Varne — the Varne, that curious, long, steep hill, with its twin ridge close by, the Colbert; they stand right up in the Channel between France and England; they very nearly lift their heads above the waves. I passed over the crest of them, unknowing, into the deep beyond, and still the ship raced on. Then, somewhat suddenly, so suddenly that I gave a cry, I saw right up above me, through what was now a thick haze, the cliffs of England, perhaps two miles away, and showing very faintly indeed, a bare outline upon the white weather. A thought ran into my mind with violence, how, one behind the other, beyond known things, beyond history, the men from whom I came had greeted this sight after winds like these and danger and the crossing of the narrow seas. I looked at my watch; it was ten o'clock, so that this crossing had taken three hours, and to see the land again like that was better than any harbour, and I knew that all those hours my mind had been at strain. I looked again at the vague cliffs narrowly, thinking them the South Foreland, but as they cleared I saw to my astonishment that I had blown all down the Straits, and that Folkestone and the last walls of the chalk were before me.

The wind dropped; the sea went on uneasily, tumbling and rolling, but within a very little while—before eleven, I think—there was no breeze at all; and there I lay, with Folkestone harbour not a mile away, but never any chance of getting there; and I whistled, but no wind came. I sat idle and admired the loneliness of the sea. Till, towards one, a little draught of air blew slantwise from the land, and under it I crept to the smooth water within the stone arm of the breakwater, and there I let the anchor go, and, settling everything, I slept.

It is pleasant to remember these things.

THE VALLEY OF THE ROTHER

THERE is in that part of England which is very properly called her Eden (that centre of all good things and home of happy men, the county of Sussex), there is, I say, in that exalted county a valley which I shall praise for your greater pleasure, because I know that it is too jealously guarded for any run of strangers to make it common, and because I am very sure that you may go and only make it the more delightful by your presence It is the valley of the River Rother; the sacred and fruitful river between the downs and the weald.

Now here many travelling men, bicyclists even and some who visit for a livelihood, will think I mean the famous River Rother that almost reaches the sea. The Rother into which the foreigners sailed for so many hundred years, the River of the Marshes, the river on which stands Rye; the easy Rother along whose deep meadows are the sloping kilns, the bright tiled towns and the steep roads; the red Rother that is fed by streams from the ironstone. This Rother also all good men know and love, both those that come in for pleasure, strangers of Kent, and those that have a distant birthright in East Sussex, being born beyond Ouse in the Rape of Bramber.

But it is not this Rother that I am telling of, though I would love to tell of it also—as indeed I would love to tell at length of all the rivers of Sussex—the Brede, the Ouse, the Adur, the Cuckmere; all the streams that cut the chalk hills. But for this I have no space and you no patience. Neither can I tell you of a thousand adventures and wonderful hazards along the hills and valley of this eastern Rother; of how I once through a telescope on Brightling Hill saw the meet at Battle, and of how it looked quite near; of how I leapt the River Rother once, landing on the far side safely (which argues the river narrow or the leap tremendous); of how I poached in the wood of a friend who is still my friend; of how I rode a horse into Robertsbridge; of the inn. All these things could I tell with growing fervour, and to all these would you listen with an increasing delight. But I must write of the River Rother under Petworth, the other Rother in the West. Why? Because I started out so to do, and no man should let himself be led away by a word, or by any other such little thing.

Let me therefore have done with this eastern river, far away from my home, a river at the end of long journeys, and speak of that other noble Rother, the Rother of quiet men, the valley that is like a shrine in England.

Many famous towns and villages stand in the valley of this river and even (some of them) upon its very banks. Thus there are the three principal towns of this part, Midhurst and Petworth and Pulborough: but these have been dealt with and written of in so many great books and by such a swarm of new men, that I have no business further to describe their merits and antiquity. But this I will add to all that is known of them. Midhurst takes its name from standing in the middle, for it is half way between the open downs and the thick woods on the borders of Surrey. Petworth has a steeple that slopes to one side; not so much as Chesterfield, but somewhat more than most steeples. Pulborough stands upon a hill, and is famous for its corn-market, to which people come from far and near, from as far off as Burpham or as close by as Bury. All these noble towns have (as I said before) been written of in books, only no book that I know puts them all together and calls them "the Valley of the Rother." That is the title that such a book should have if it is to treat of the heart of West Sussex, and I make no doubt that such a book would be read lovingly by many men.

For the Valley of the Rother breeds men and is

the cause of many delightful villages, all the homes
of men. I know that Cobden was born there, the
last of the yeomen : I hope that Cobbett lived here
too. Manning was here in his short married life;
he lived at Barlton (which foolish men call Bar-
lavington), under the old Downs, where the steep
woods make a hollow. In this valley also are
Fittleworth (the only place in England that rhymes
with Little Worth) ; Duncton, about which there
is nothing to be said ; Burton, which is very old
and has its church right in the grounds of the
house ; West-burton, where the racehorses were ;
Graffham, Bignor, Sutton, and I know not how
many delightful hamlets.

In the Valley of the River Rother no hurried
men ever come, for it leads nowhere. They cross
it now and then, and they forget it ; but who, unless
he be a son or a lover, has really known that
plain ? It leads nowhere : to the no man's land,
the broken country by Liss. It has in it no curious
sight, but only beauty. The rich men in it (and
thank Heaven they are few) are of a reticent
and homing kind, or (when the worst comes to
the worst) they have estates elsewhere, and go north
for their pleasure.

Foxes are hunted in the Valley of the Rother, but
there are not very many. Pheasants and partridges
are shot, but I never heard of great bags ; one
animal indeed there is in profusion. The rabbit

swarms and exults in this life of Southern England.
Do you stalk him? He sits and watches you.
Do you hunt him with dogs? He thinks it a vast
pother about a very little matter. Do you ferret
him? He dies, and rejoices to know that so many
more will take his place. The rabbit is the sacred
emblem of my river, and when we have a symbol,
he shall be our symbol. He loves men and eats
the things they plant, especially the tender shoots
of young trees, wheat, and the choice roots in
gardens. He only remains, and is happy all his
little life in the valley from which we depart when
our boyhood ends.

The Valley of the Rother is made of many parts.
There is the chalk of the Southern Down-land,
the belt of the loam beneath it; then the curious
country of sand, full of dells and dark with pine
woods; then the luxurious meadows, which are
open and full of cattle, colts, and even sheep;
then the woods. It is, in a few miles, a little
England. There are also large heaths—larger, you
would think, than such a corner of the earth could
contain; old elms and oaks; many wide parks;
fish ponds; one trout stream and half a score of
mills. There are men of many characters, but all
happy, honest, good, witty, and hale. And when
I have said all I could say of this delightful place
(which indeed I think is set apart for the reward of
virtue) I should not have given you a tithe of its

prosperity and peace and beneficence. There is the picture of the Valley of the River Rother. It flows in a short and happy murmur from the confined hills by Hindhead to the Arun itself; but of the Arun no one could write with any justice except at the expense of far more space and time than I have given me.

If ever again we have a religion in the South Country, we will have a temple to my darling valley. It shall be round, with columns and a wall, and there I will hang a wreath in thanksgiving for having known the river.

THE CORONATION

MY companion said to me that there was a doom over the day and the reign and the times, and that the turn of the nation had come. He felt it in the sky.

The day had been troubled: from the forest ridge to the sea there was neither wind nor sun, but a dull, even heat oppressed the fields and the high downs under an uncertain, half-luminous confusion of grey clouds. It was as though a relief was being denied, and as though something inexorable had come into that air which is normally the softest and most tender in the world. The hours of the low tide were too silent. The little inland river was quite dead, the reeds beside it dry and motionless; even in the trees about it no leaves stirred.

In the late afternoon, as the heat grew more masterful, a slight wind came out of the east. It was so faint and doubtful in quantity that one could not be certain, as one stood on the deserted shore, whether it blew from just off the land or from the sullen level of the sea. It followed along the line of the coast without refreshment and without vigour, even hotter than had been the still air out of which it was engendered. It did not do more than ruffle here and there the uneasy surface of our sea ; that surface moved a little, but with a motion borrowed from nothing so living or so natural as the wind. It was a dull memory of past storms, or perhaps that mysterious heaving from the lower sands which sailors know, but which no science has yet explained.

In such an influence of expectation and of pre-sage—an influence having in it that quality which seemed to the ancients only Fate, but to us moderns a something evil—in the strained atten-tion for necessary and immovable things that can-not hear and cannot pity—the hour came for me to reascend the valley to my home. Already upon the far and confused horizon two or three motion-less sails that had been invisible began to show white against a rising cloud. This cloud had not the definition of sudden conquering storms, proper to the summer, and leaving a blessing behind their fury. The edge of it against the misty and brooding sky had all the vagueness of smoke, and as it rose up out of the sea its growth was so methodical and regular as to disconnect it wholly in one's mind from the little fainting breeze that still blew, from rain, or from any daily thing. It advanced with the fall of the evening till it held half the sky. There it seemed halted for a while, and lent by contrast an unnatural brightness to

the parched hills beneath it ; for now the sun having set, we had come north of the gap, and were
looking southward upon that spectacle as upon
the climax of a tragedy. But there was nothing of
movement or of sound. No lightning, no thunder;
and soon the hot breath of the afternoon had itself
disappeared before the advance of this silent pall.
The night of June to the north was brighter than
twilight, and still southward, a deliberate spectacle,
stood this great range of vague and menacing
cloud, shutting off the sky and towering above the
downs, so that it seemed permissible to ascribe to
those protecting gods of our valley a burden of fear.

Just when all that scene had been arranged to
an adjustment that no art could have attained, the
first great fire blazed out miles and miles to the
west, somewhere above Midhurst : I think near No
Man's Land. Then we saw, miles to the east
again, a glare over Mount Harry, the signal of
Lewes, and one after another all the heights took
it up in a chain—above Bramber, above Poynings,
above Wiston, on Amberley Mount (I think), certainly on the noble sweep of Bury. Even in those
greater distances which the horizon concealed they
were burning and answering each other into
Hampshire : perhaps on the beaten grass of the
high forts above Portsmouth, and to the left away
to the flat Rye level, and to the eastern Rother ; for
we saw the line of red angry upon that cloud

which had come to receive it, an endless line which suddenly called up what one had heard old men say of the prairie fires.

It was easy, without covering the face and without abstracting the mind from the whirl of modern circumstance, it was easy, merely looking at the thing, to be seized with an impression of disaster. The stars were so pale on the lingering white light of the pure north, the smoky cloud so deep and heavy and steadfast and low above the hills, the fire so near to it, so sharp against it, and so huge, that the awe and sinister meaning of conflagrations dominated the impression of all the scene. There arose in the mind that memory which associates such a glare and the rising and falling fury of flames with sacrifice or with vengeance, or with the warning of an enemy's approach, or with the mark of his conquest ; for with such things our race (for how many thousand years !) has watched the fires upon the hills far off. It touched one as does the reiterated note of a chaunt ; if not with an impression of doom, at least with that of calamity.

When the fires had died down to a sullen glow, and the men watching them had gone home under the weight of what they had seen, the storm broke and occupied the whole sky. A very loud wind rose and a furious rain fell. It became suddenly cold ; there was thunder all over the weald, and the lightning along the unseen crest of the downs answered the lightning above the forest.

THE MEN OF THE DESERT

I LAY once alone upon the crest of a range
whose name I have never seen spelt, but which
is pronounced "Haueedja," from whence a man
can see right away for ever the expanse of the
Sahara.

It is well known that Mount Atlas and those
inhabited lands where there is a sufficient rainfall
and every evidence of man's activity, the Province
of Africa, the plateaux which are full of the
memories of Rome, end abruptly towards the sun,
and are bounded by a sort of cliff which falls sheer
upon the desert. On the summit of this cliff I lay
and looked down upon the sand. It was impressed
upon my mind that here was an influence quite
peculiar, not to be discovered in any other climate
of the world ; that all Europe received that influence, and yet that no one in Europe had accepted
it save for his hurt.

God forbid that any man should pretend that the
material environment of mankind determines the
destiny of mankind. Those who say such things
have abandoned the domain of intelligence. But

it is true that the soul eagerly seeks for and receives the impressions of the world about it, and will be moved to a different creed or to a different poetry, according as the body perceives the sea or the hills or the rainless and inhuman places which lie to the south of Europe ; and certainly the souls of those races which have inhabited the great zone of calms between the trade winds and the tropics, those races which have felt nothing beneficent, but only something awful and unfamiliar in the earth and sky, have produced a peculiar philosophy.

It is to be remarked that this philosophy is not atheist; those races called Semitic have never denied either the presence or the personality of God.   It is, on the contrary, their boast that they have felt His presence, His unity, and His person- ality in a manner more pointed than have the rest of mankind ; and those of us who pretend to find in the Desert a mere negation, are checked by the thought that within the Desert the most positive of religions have appeared.   Indeed, to deny God has been the sad privilege of very few in any society of men ; and those few, if it be examined, have invariably been men in whom the power to experience was deadened, usually by luxury, sometimes by distress.

It is not atheist ; but whatever it is, it is hurtful, and has about it something of the despair and strength of atheism.   Consider the Book of Job ;

consider the Arab Mohammedan ; consider the
fierce heresies which besieged the last of the
Romans in this Province of Africa, and which
tortured the short history of the Vandals ; consider
the modern tragedies which develop among the
French soldiers to the north and to the south of
this wide belt of sand ; and you will see that the
thing which the Sahara and its prolongation produce is something evil, or at least to us evil.
There is in the idea running through the mind
of the Desert an intensity which may be of some
value to us if it be diluted by a large admixture of
European tradition, or if it be mellowed and transformed by a long process of time, but which, if
we take it at its source and inspire ourselves
directly from it, warps and does hurt to our European sense.

It may be taken that whatever form truth takes
among men will be the more perfect in proportion
as the men who receive that form are more fully
men. The whole of truth can never be comprehended by anything finite ; and truth as it
appears to this species or to that is most true when
the type which receives it is the healthiest and the
most normal of its own kind. The truth as it is to
men is most true when the men who receive it are
the healthiest and the most normal of men. We
in Europe are the healthiest and most normal of
our kind. It is to us that the world must look for

its headship; we have the harbours, the continual presence of the sea through all our polities; we have that high differentiation between the various parts of our unity which makes the whole of Europe so marvellous an organism; we alone change without suffering decay. To the truth as Europe accepts it I cannot but bow down; for if that is not the truth, then the truth is not to be found upon earth. But there comes upon us perpetually that "wind of Africa"; and it disturbs us. As I lay that day, a year ago, upon the crest of the mountain, my whole mind was possessed with the influence of such a gale.

Day after day, after day, the silent men of the Desert go forward across its monotonous horizons; their mouths are flanked with those two deep lines of patience and of sorrow which you may note to-day in all the ghettoes of Europe; their smile, when they smile, is restrained by a sort of ironic strength in the muscles of the face. Their eyes are more bright than should be eyes of happy men; they are, as it were, inured to sterility; there is nothing in them of that repose which we Westerners acquire from a continual contemplation of deep pastures and of innumerable leaves; they are at war, not only among themselves, but against the good earth; in a silent and powerful way they are also *afraid*.

You may note that their morals are an angry

series of unexplained commands, and that their worship does not include that fringe of half-reasonable, wholly pleasing things which the true worship of a true God must surely contain. All is as clear-cut as their rocks, and as unfruitful as their dry valleys, and as dreadful as their brazen sky; "thou shalt not" this, that, and the other. Their god is jealous; he is vengeful; he is (awfully present and real to them!) a vision of that demon of which we in our happier countries make a quaint legend. He catches men out and trips them up; he has but little relation to the Father of Christian men, who made the downs of South England and the high clouds above them.

The good uses of the world are forgotten in the Desert, or fiercely denied. Love is impure; so are birth, and death, and eating, and every other necessary part in the life of a man. And yet, though all these things are impure, there is no lustration. We also feel in a genial manner that this merry body of ours requires apology; but those others to the south of us have no toleration in their attitude; they are awfully afraid.

I have continually considered, as I have read my history, the special points in which their influence is to be observed in the development of Europe. It takes the form of the great heresies; the denial of the importance of matter (sometimes of its existence); the denial that anything but matter exists; the denial of the family; the denial of ownership; the over-simplicity which is peculiarly a Desert product runs through all such follies, as does the rejection of a central and governing power upon earth, which is again just such a rebellion as the Desert would bring. I say the great heresies are the main signs of that influence; but it is in small and particular matters that you may see its effect most clearly.

For instance, the men of the Desert are afraid of wine. They have good reason; if you drink wine in the Desert you die. In the Desert, a man can drink only water; and, when he gets it, it is like diamonds to him, or, better still, it is like rejuvenation. All our long European legends which denounce and bring a curse upon the men who are the enemies of wine, are legends inspired by our hatred of the thing which is not Europe, and that bounds Europe, and is the enemy of Europe.

So also with their attachment to numbers. For instance, the seventh day must have about it something awful and oppressive; the fast must be seven times seven days, and so forth. We Europeans have always smiled in our hearts at these things. We would take this day or that, and make up a scheme of great and natural complexity, full of interlacing seasons; and nearly all our special days were days of rejoicing. We carried images about our fields further to develop and enhance the nature of our religion; we dedicated trees and caves; and the feasts of one place were not the feasts of another. But to the men of the Desert mere unfruitful number was a god.

Then again, the word, especially the written word, the document, overshadows their mind. It has always had for them a power of something mysterious. To engrave characters was to cast a spell; and when they seek for some infallible authority upon earth, they can only discover it in the written characters traced in a sacred book. All their expression of worship is wrought through symbols. With us, the symbol is clearly retained separate from that for which it stands, though hallowed by that for which it stands. With them the symbol is the whole object of affection.

On this account you will find in the men of the Desert a curious panic in the presence of statues, which is even more severe than the panic they suffer in the presence of wine. It is as though they said to themselves: "Take this away; if you leave it here I shall worship it." They are subject to possession.

Side by side with this fear of the graphic representation of men or of animals, you will find in them an incapacity to represent them well. The art of the iconoclasts is either childish, weak, or, at its strongest, evil.

And especially among all these symptoms of
the philosophy from which they suffer is their
manner of comprehending the nature of creation.
Of creation in any form they are afraid ; and the
infinite Creator is on that account present to them
almost as though He were a man, for when we are
afraid of things we see them very vividly indeed.
On this account you will find in the legends of
the men of the Desert all manner of fantastic
tales incomprehensible to us Europeans, wherein
God walks, talks, eats, and wrestles. Nor is there
any trace in this attitude of theirs of parable or of
allegory. That mixture of the truth, and of a subtle
unreal glamour which expands and confirms the
truth, is a mixture proper to our hazy landscapes,
to our drowsy woods, and to our large vision.
We, who so often see from our high village
squares soft and distant horizons, mountains now
near, now very far, according as the weather
changes : we, who are perpetually feeling the
transformation of the seasons, and who are im-
mersed in a very ocean of manifold and mysterious
life, we need, create, and live by legends. The
line between the real and the imaginary is vague
and penumbral to us. We are justly influenced
by our twilights, and our imagination teaches us.
How many deities have we not summoned up to
inhabit groves and lakes—special deities who are
never seen, but yet have never died ?

To the men of the Desert, doubt and beauty mingled in this fashion seemed meaningless. That which they worship they see and almost handle. In the dreadful silence which surrounds them, their illusions turn into convictions—the haunting voices are heard : the forms are seen.

Of two further things, native to us, their starved experience has no hold ; of nationality (or, if the term be preferred, of "The City") and of what we have come to call "chivalry." The two are but aspects of one thing without a name ; but that thing all Europeans possess, nor is it possible for us to conceive of a patriotism unless it is a patriotism which is chivalric. In our earliest stories, we honour men fighting odds. Our epics are of small numbers against great ; humility and charity are in them, lending a kind of magic strength to the sword. The Faith did not bring in that spirit, but rather completed it. Our boundaries have always been intensely sacred to us. We are not passionate to cross them save for the sake of adventure ; but we are passionate to defend them. In all that enormous story of Rome, from the dim Etrurian origins right up to the end of her thousand years, the Wall of the Town was more sacred than the limits of the Empire.

The men of the Desert do not understand these things. They are by compulsion nomad, and for ever wandering ; they strike no root ; their pride is in a mere expansion ; they must colonize or fail ; nor does any man die for a city.

As I looked from the mountain, I thought the Desert which I had come so far to see had explained to me what hitherto I had not understood in the mischances of Europe. I remained for a long while looking out upon the glare.

But when I came down again, northward from the high sandstone hill, and was in the fields again near running water, and drinking wine from a cup carved with Roman emblems, I began to wonder whether the Desert had not put before my mind, as they say it can do before the eye of the traveller, a mirage.

Is there such an influence? Are there such men ?

THE DEPARTURE

ONCE, in Barbary, I grew tired of unusual things, especially of palms, and desired to return to Europe and the things I knew ; so I went down from the hills to the sea coast, and when after two days I had reached the railway, I took a train for Algiers and reached that port at evening.

From Algiers it is possible to go at once and for almost any sum one chooses to any part of the world. The town is on the sharp slope of a theatre of hills, and in the quiet harbour below it there are all sorts of ships, but mostly steamships, moored with their sterns towards the quay. For there is no tide here, and the ships can lie quite still.

I sat upon a wall of the upper town and considered how each of these ships was going to some different place, and how pleasant it was to roam about the world. Behind the ships, along the stone quays, were a great number of wooden huts, of offices built into archways, of little houses, booths, and dens, in each of which you could take your passage to some place or other.

"Now," said I to myself, "now is the time to be free." For one never feels master of oneself unless one is obeying no law, plan, custom, trend, or necessity, but simply spreading out at ease and occupying the world. In this also Aristotle was misled by fashion, or was ill-informed by some friend of his, or was, perhaps, lying for money when he said that liberty was obedience to a self-made law; for the most distant hint of law is odious to liberty. True, it is more free to obey a law of one's own making than of some one else's; just as if a man should give himself a punch in the eye it would be less hurtful and far less angering than one given by a passer-by; yet to suffer either would not be a benefit of freedom. Liberty cannot breathe where the faintest odour of regulation is to be discovered, but only in that ether whose very nature is largeness. Oh! Diviner Air! how few have drunk you, and in what deep draughts have I !

I had a great weight of coined, golden, metallic money all loose in my pocket. There was no call upon me nor any purpose before me. I spent an hour looking down upon the sea and the steamships, and taking my pick out of all the world.

One thing, however, guided me, which was this: that desire, to be satisfied at all, must be satisfied at once ; and of the many new countries I might seek that would most attract me whose ship was starting soonest. So I looked round for mooring cables in the place of anchor chains, for Blue Peter, for smoke from funnels, for little boats coming and going, and for all that shows a steam-boat to be off; when I saw, just behind a large new boat in such a condition of bustle, a sign in huge yellow letters staring on a bright black ground, which said : "To the Balearic Islands, eight shillings"; underneath, in smaller yellow letters, was written : "Gentlemen The Honour-able Travellers are warned that they must pay for any food they consume." When I had read this notice I said to myself : " I will go to the Balearic Islands, of which the rich have never heard. I, poor and unencumbered, will go and visit these remote places, which have in their time received all the influences of the world, and which yet have no history ; for I am tired of this Africa, where so many men are different from me." As I said this to myself I saw a little picture in my mind of three small islands standing in the middle of the sea, quite alone, and inhabited by happy men ; but this picture, as it always is with such pictures, was not at all the same as what I saw when next morning the islands rose along the north to which we steered.

I went down to the quay by some large stone

steps which an Englishman had built many years
ago, and I entered the office above which this
great sign was raised.   Within was a tall man of
doubtful race, smoking a cigarette made of loose
paper, and gazing kindly at the air.   He was full
of reveries.   Of this man I asked when the boat
would be starting.   He told me it started in half
an hour, a little before the setting of the sun.   So
I bought a ticket for eight shillings, upon which
it was clearly printed in two languages that I had
bound myself to all manner of things by the purchase, and especially that I might not go below,
but must sit upon deck all night; nevertheless,
I was glad to hold that little bit of printed prose,
for it would enable me to reach the Balearic
Islands, which for all other men are names in a
dream.   I then went up into the town of Algiers,
and was careful to buy some ham from a Jew,
some wine from a Mohammedan, and some bread
and chocolate from a very indifferent Christian.
After that I got aboard.   As I came over the side
I heard the sailors, stokers, and people all talking
to each other in low tones, and I at once recognized the tongue called Catalan.

I had heard this sort of Latin in many places,
some lonely and some populous.   I had heard it
once from a chemist at Perpignan who dressed a
wound of mine, and this was the first time I heard
it. Very often after in the valleys of the Pyrenees,

in the Cerdagne, and especially in Andorra, hundreds of men had spoken to me in Catalan. At Urgel, that notable city where there is only one shop and where the streets are quite narrow and Moorish, a woman and six or seven men had spoken Catalan to me for nearly one hour : it was in a cellar surrounded by great barrels, and I remember it well. So, also, on the River Noguera, coming up again into the hills, a girl who took the toll at the wooden bridge had spoken Catalan to me. But none of these had I ever answered so that they could understand, and on this account I was very grieved to hear the Catalan tongue, though I remembered that if I spoke to them with ordinary Spanish words or in French with a strong Southern accent they would usually have some idea of what I was saying.

As the evening fell the cables were slipped without songs, and with great dignity, rapidity, and order the ship was got away.

I knew a man once, a seafaring man, a Scotchman, with whom I travelled on a very slow old boat in the Atlantic, who told me that the Northern people of Europe were bravest in an unexpected danger, but the Southern in a danger long foreseen. He said he had known many of both kinds, and had served under them and commanded them. He said that in sudden accident the Northerner was the more reliable man, but that if an act of great danger had to be planned and coolly achieved, then the Southerner was strongest in doing what he had to do. He said that in taking the ground he would rather have a Northern, but in bringing in a short ship a Southern crew.

He was a man who observed closely, and never said a thing because he had read it. Indeed, he did not read, and he had in a little hanging shelf above his bunk only four or five tattered books, and even these were magazines. I remembered his testimony now as I watched these Catalans letting the ship go free, and I believed it, comparing it with history and the things I had myself seen. They did everything with such regularity and so silently that it was a different deck from what one would have had in the heave of the Channel. With Normans or Bretons, or Cornishmen or men of Kent, but especially with men from London river, there would have been all sorts of cursing and bellowing, and they could not have touched a rope without throwing themselves into attitudes of violence. But these men took the sea quite quietly, nor could you tell from their faces which was rich and which was poor.

It was not till the ship was out throbbing swiftly over the smooth sea and darkness had fallen that they began to sing. Then those of them who were not working gathered together with a stringed instrument forward and sang of

pity and of death. One of them said to me,
"Knight, can your grace sing?" I told him that
I could sing, certainly, but that my singing was
unpleasing, and that I only knew foreign songs.
He said that singing was a great solace, and
desired to hear a song of my own country. So I
sang them a song out of Sussex, to which they
listened in deep silence, and when it was con-
cluded their leader snapped and twanged at the
strings again and began another song about the
riding of horses in the hills.

So we passed the short night until the sky
upon our quarter grew faintly pale and the little
wind that rises before morning awakened the sea.

THE IDEA OF A PILGRIMAGE

A PILGRIMAGE is, of course, an expedition to some venerated place to which a vivid memory of sacred things experienced, or a long and wonderful history of human experience in divine matters, or a personal attraction affecting the soul impels one. This is, I say, its essence. So a pilgrimage may be made to the tomb of Descartes, in Paris, or it may be a little walk uphill to a neighbouring and beloved grave, or a modern travel, even in luxury, on the impulse to see something that greatly calls one.

But there has always hung round the idea of a pilgrimage, with all people and at all times—I except those very rare and highly decadent generations of history in which no pilgrimages are made, nor any journeys, save for curiosity or greed— there has always hung round it, I say, something more than the mere objective. Just as in general worship you will have noble gowns, vivid colour, and majestic music (symbols, but necessary symbols of the great business you are at); so, in this particular case of worship, clothes, as it were,

264

and accoutrements, gather round one's principal
action. I will visit the grave of a saint or of a
man whom I venerate privately for his virtues and
deeds, but on my way I wish to do something a
little difficult to show at what a price I hold communion with his resting-place, and also on the way
I will see all I can of men and things; for anything great and worthy is but an ordinary thing
transfigured, and if I am about to venerate a
humanity absorbed into the divine, so it behoves
me on my journey to it to enter into and delight in
the divine that is hidden in everything. Thus I
may go upon a pilgrimage with no pack and
nothing but a stick and my clothes, but I must get
myself into the frame of mind that carries an invisible burden, an eye for happiness and suffering,
humour, gladness at the beauty of the world, a
readiness for raising the heart at the vastness of
a wide view, and especially a readiness to give
multitudinous praise to God; for a man that goes
on a pilgrimage does best of all if he starts out (I
say it of his temporal object only) with the heart
of a wanderer, eager for the world as it is, forget-
ful of maps or descriptions, but hungry for real
colours and men and the seeming of things. This
desire for reality and contact is a kind of humility,
this pleasure in it a kind of charity.

It is surely in the essence of a pilgrimage that
all vain imaginations are controlled by the great-

ness of our object.   Thus, if a man should go to
see the place where (as they say) St. Peter met our
Lord on the Appian Way at dawn, he will not care
very much for the niggling of pedants about this
or that building, or for the rhetoric of posers about
this or that beautiful picture.   If a thing in his
way seem to him frankly ugly he will easily treat
it as a neutral, forget it and pass it by.   If, on the
contrary, he find a beautiful thing, whether done
by God or by man, he will remember and love it.
This is what children do, and to get the heart of a
child is the end surely of any act of religion.   In
such a temper he will observe rather than read,
and though on his way he cannot do other than
remember the names of places, saying, " Why,
these are the Alps of which I have read!   Here
is Florence, of which I have heard so many rich
women talk!" yet he will never let himself argue
and decide or put himself, so to speak, before an
audience in his own mind—for that is pride which
all of us moderns always fall into.   He will, on
the contrary, go into everything with curiosity
and pleasure, and be a brother to the streets and
trees and to all the new world he finds.   The Alps
that he sees with his eyes will be as much more
than the names he read about, the Florence of his
desires as much more than the Florence of sickly
drawing-rooms; as beauty loved is more than
beauty heard of, or as our own taste, smell, hearing,

touch and sight are more than the vague relations of others. Nor does religion exercise in our common life any function more temporarily valuable than this, that it makes us be sure at least of realities, and look very much askance at philosophies and imaginaries and academic whimsies.

Look, then, how a pilgrimage ought to be nothing but a nobler kind of travel, in which, according to our age and inclination, we tell our tales, or draw our pictures, or compose our songs. It is a very great error, and one unknown before our most recent corruptions, that the religious spirit should be so superficial and so self-conscious as to dominate our method of action at special times and to be absent at others. It is better occasionally to travel in one way or another to some beloved place (or to some place wonderful and desired for its associations), haunted by our mission, yet falling into every ordinary levity, than to go about a common voyage in a chastened and devout spirit. I fear this is bad theology, and I propound it subject to authority. But, surely, if a man should say, " I will go to Redditch to buy needles cheap," and all the way take care to speak no evil of his neighbour, to keep very sober, to be punctual in his accounts, and to say his regular prayers with exactitude, though that would be a good work, yet if he is to be a *pilgrim* (and the Church has a hundred gates), I would rather for the moment that he went off in a gay, tramping spirit, not over-sure of his expenses, not very careful of all he said or did, but illuminated and increasingly informed by the great object of his voyage, which is here not to buy or sell needles, or what not, but to loose the mind and purge it in the ultimate contemplation of something divine.

There is, indeed, that kind of pilgrimage which some few sad men undertake because their minds are overburdened by a sin or tortured with some great care that is not of their own fault. These are excepted from the general rule, though even to these a very human spirit comes by the way, and the adventures of inns and foreign conversations broaden the world for them and lighten their burden. But this kind of pilgrimage is rare and special, having its peculiar virtues. The common sort (which how many men undertake under another name!) is a separate and human satisfaction of a need, the fulfilling of an instinct in us, the realization of imagined horizons, the reaching of a goal. For whoever yet that was alive reached an end and could say he was satisfied? Yet who has not desired so to reach an end and to be satisfied? Well, pilgrimage is for the most a sort of prefiguring or rehearsal. A man says: "I will play in show (but a show stiffened with a real and just object) at that great part which is all we can ever play. Here I start from home, and there I reach a goal, and on the way I laugh and watch, sing and work. Now I am at ease and again hampered ; now poor, now rich, weary towards the end and at last arrived at that end. So my great life is, and so this little chapter shall be." Thus he packs up the meaning of life into a little space to be able to look at it closely, as men carry with them small locket portraits of their birthplace or of those they love.

If a pilgrimage is all this, it is evident that, however careless, it must not be untroublesome. It would be a contradiction of pilgrimage to seek to make the journey short and vapid, merely consuming the mind for nothing, as is our modern habit; for they seem to think nowadays that to remain as near as possible to what one was at starting, and to one's usual rut, is the great good of travel (as though a man should run through the *Iliad* only to note the barbarous absurdity of the Greek characters, or through Catullus for the sake of discovering such words as were like enough to English). That is not the spirit of a pilgrimage at all. The pilgrim is humble and devout, and human, and charitable, and ready to smile and admire ; therefore he should comprehend the whole of his way, the people in it, and the hills and the clouds, and the habits of the various cities. And as to the method of doing this, we may go bicycling (though that is a little flurried) or driving (though that is luxurious and dangerous, because it brings us constantly against servants and flattery); but the best way of all is on foot, where one is a man like any other man, with the sky above one, and the road beneath, and the world on every side, and time to see all.

So also I designed to walk, and did, when I visited the tombs of the Apostles.

THE ARENA

IT was in Paris, in his room on the hill of the University, that a traveller woke and wondered what he should do with his day. In some way—I cannot tell how—ephemeral things had captured his mind in the few hours he had already spent in the city. There is no civilization where the various parts stand so separate as they do with the French. You may live in Paris all your life and never suspect that there is a garrison of eighty thousand men within call. You may spend a year in a provincial town and never hear that the large building you see daily is a bishop's palace. Or you may be the guest of the bishop for a month, and remain under the impression that somewhere, hidden away in the place, there is a powerful clique of governing atheists whom, somehow, you never run across. And so this traveller, who knew Paris like his pocket, and had known it since he could speak plain, had managed to gather up in this particular visit all the impressions which are least characteristic of the town. He had dined with a friend at Pousset's ; he had passed the evening at the Exhibition, and he had had a bare touch of the

real thing in the Rue de Tournon ; but even there
it was in the company of foreigners.   Therefore, I
repeat, he woke up next morning wondering what
he should do, for the veneer of Paris is the thin-
nest in the world, and he had exhausted it in one
feverish day.

Luckily for him, the room in which he lay was
French, and had been French for a hundred years.
You looked out of window into a sky cut by the
tall Mansard roofs of the eighteenth century ; and
over the stones of what had been the Scotch Col-
lege you could see below you at the foot of the hill
all the higher points of the island—especially the
Sainte Chapelle and the vast towers of the cathedral.   Then it suddenly struck him that the air
was full of bells.   Now, it is a curious thing, and
one that every traveller will bear me out in, that
you associate a country place with the sound of
bells, but a capital never.   Caen is noisy enough
and Rouen big enough, one would think, to drown
the memory of music ; yet any one who has lived
in his Normandy remembers their perpetual bells;
and as for the admirable town of Chinon, where
no one ever goes, I believe it is Ringing Island
itself.   But Paris one never thinks of as a place
of bells.   And yet there are bells enough there
to take a man right into the past, and from there
through fairyland to hell and out and back again.

.   .   .   .   .   .

If I were writing of the bells, I could make you a list of all the famous bells, living and dead, that haunt the city, and the tale of what they have done would be a history of France. The bell of the St. Bartholomew over against the Louvre, the tocsin of the Hotel de Ville that rang the knell of the Monarchy, the bell of St. Julien that is as old as the University, the old Bourdon of Notre Dame that first rang when St. Louis brought in the crown of thorns, and the peal that saluted Napoleon, and the new Bourdon that is made of the guns of Sebastopol, and the Savoyarde up on Montmartre, a new bell much larger than the rest. This morning the air was full of them. They came up to the height on which the traveller lay listening; they came clear and innumerable over the distant surge of the streets; he spent an hour wondering at such an unusual Parliament and General Council of Bells. Then he said to himself: "It must be some great feast of the Church." He was in a world he had never known before. He was like a man who gets into a strange country in a dream and follows his own imagination instead of suffering the pressure of outer things; or like a boy who wanders by a known river till he comes to unknown gardens.

So anxious was he to take possession at once of this discovery of his that he went off hurriedly without eating or drinking, thinking only of what

he might find.   He desired to embrace at one sight
all that Paris was doing on a day which was full
of St. Louis and of resurrection.   The thoughts
upon thoughts that flow into the mind from its
impression, as water creams up out of a stone
fountain at a river head, disturbed him, swelling
beyond the possibility of fulfilment.   He wished
to see at once the fashionables in St. Clotilde and
the Greek Uniates at St. Julien, and the
empty Sorbonne and the great crowd of boys at
Stanislas ; but what he was going to see never
occurred to him, for he thought he knew Paris too
well to approach the cathedral.

Notre Dame is jealously set apart for special and
well-advertised official things.   If you know the
official world you know the great church, and
unless some great man had died, or some victory
had been won, you would never go there to see
how Paris took its religion.   No midnight Mass is
said in it ; for the lovely carols of the Middle Ages
you must go to St. Gervais, and for the pomp
of the Counter-Reformation to the Madeleine,
for soldiers to St. Augustin, for pilgrims to
St. Etienne.   Therefore no one would ever have
thought of going to the cathedral on this day,
when an instinct and revelation of Paris at prayer
filled the mind.   Nevertheless, the traveller's feet
went, of their own accord, towards the seven
bridges, because the Island draws all Paris to it,

and was drawing him along with the rest. He had meant perhaps to go the way that all the world has gone since men began to live on this river, and to follow up the Roman way across the Seine —a vague intention of getting a Mass at St. Merry or St. Laurent. But he was going as a dream sent him, without purpose or direction.

The sun was already very hot, and the Parvis was blinding with light when he crossed the little bridge. Then he noticed that the open place had dotted about it little groups of people making eastward. The Parvis is so large that you could have a multitude scattered in it and only notice that the square was not deserted. There were no more than a thousand, perhaps, going separately towards Notre Dame, and a thousand made no show in such a square. But when he went in through the doors he saw there something he had never seen before, and that he thought did not exist. It was as though the vague interior visions of which the morning had been so full had taken on reality.

You may sometimes see in modern picture galleries an attempt to combine the story from which proceeds the nourishing flame of Christianity with the crudities and the shameful ugliness of our decline. Thus, with others, a picture of our Lord and Mary Magdalen; all the figures except that of our Lord were dressed in the modern way. I remember another of our Lord and the little children, where the scene is put into a village school. Now, if you can imagine (which it is not easy to do) such an attempt to be successful, untouched by the love of display and eccentricity, and informing—as it commonly pretends to inform —our time with an idea, then you will understand what the traveller saw that morning in Notre Dame. The church seemed the vastest cavern that had ever been built for worship. Coming in from the high morning, the half-light alone, with which we always connect a certain majesty and presence, seemed to have taken on amplitude as well. The incense veiled what appeared to be an infinite lift of roof, and the third great measurement—the length of nave that leads like a forest ride to the lights of the choir—was drawn out into an immeasurable perspective by reason of a countless crowd of men and women divided by the narrow path of the procession. So full was this great place that a man moved slowly and with difficulty, edging through such a mass of folk as you may find at holiday time in a railway station, or outside a theatre—never surely before was a church like this, unless, indeed, some very rich or very famous man happened to be gracing it. But here to-day, for nothing but the function proper to the feast, the cathedral was paved and floored with human beings. In the galilee there was a kind of movement so that a man could get up further, and at last the traveller found a place to stand in just on the edge of the open gangway, at the very end of the nave. He peered up this, and saw from the further end, near the altar, the head of the procession approaching, which was (in his fancy of that morning) like the line of the Faith, still living and returning in a perpetual circle to revivify the world. Moreover, there was in the advent of the procession a kind of climax. As it came nearer, the great crowd moved more thickly towards it; children were lifted up, and by one of Sully's wide pillars a group of three young soldiers climbed on a rail to see the great sight better. The Cardinal-Archbishop, very old, and supported by his priests, half walked and half tottered down the length of the people ; his head, grown weary with age, barely supported the mitre, from which great jewels, false or true, were flashing. In his hand he had a crozier that was studded in the same way with gems, and that seemed to be made of gold ; the same hands had twisted the metal of it as had hammered the hinges of the cathedral doors. Certainly there here appeared one of the resurrections of Europe. The matter of life seemed to take on a fuller stuff and to lift into a dimension above that in which it ordinarily moves. The thin, narrow, and unfruitful experience of to-day and yesterday was amplified by all the lives that have

made our life, and the blood of which we are only
a last expression, the race that is older even than
Rome seemed in this revelation of continuity to be
gathered up into one intense and passionate
moment.   The pagan altar of Tiberius, the legend
of Dionysius, the whole circle of the wars came
into this one pageant, and the old man in his
office and his blessing was understood by all the
crowd before him to transmit the centuries.   A
rich woman thrust a young child forward, and he
stopped and stooped with difficulty to touch its
hair.   As he approached the traveller it was as
though there had come great and sudden news to
him, or the sound of unexpected and absorbing
music.

The procession went on and closed ; the High
Mass followed ; it lasted a very long time, and the
traveller went out before the crowd had moved and
found himself again in the glare of the sun on the
Parvis.   He went over the bridge to find his eat-
ing-shop near the archives, and eat the first food
of that day, thinking as he went that certainly
there are an infinity of lives side by side in our
cities, and each ignores the rest; and yet, that to
pass from what we know of these to what we do
not—though it is the most wonderful journey in
the world—is one that no one undertakes unless
accident or a good fortune pushes him on.   He
desired to make another such journey.

He came back to find me in London, and spoke to me of Paris as of a city newly discovered : as I listened I thought I saw an arena.

In a plain of the north, undistinguished by great hills, open to the torment of the sky, the gods had traced an arena wherein were to be fought out the principal battles of a later age.

.   .   .   .   .   .

Spirits lower than the divine, spirits intermediate, have been imagined by men wiser than ourselves to have some power over the world—a power which we might vanquish in a special manner, but still a power. To such conceptions the best races of Europe cling ; upon such a soil are grown the legends that tell us most about our dark, and yet enormous, human fate. These intermediate spirits have been called in all the older creeds "the gods." It is in the nature of the Church to frown upon these dreams ; but I, as I listened to him, saw clearly that plain wherein the gods had marked out an arena for mankind.

It was oval, as should be a theatre for any show, with heights around it insignificant, but offering a vantage ground whence could be watched the struggle in the midst. There was a sacred centre —an island and a mount—and, within the lines, so great a concourse of gladiatorial souls as befits the greatest of spectacles. I say, I do not know how

far such visions are permitted, nor how far the
right reason of the Church condemns them ; but
the dream returned to me very powerfully, recall-
ing my boyhood, when the traveller told me his
story.   I also therefore went and caught the fresh
gale of the stream of the Seine in flood, and saw
the many roofs of Paris quite clear after rain, and
read the writings of the men I mixed with and
heard the noise of the city.

.   .   .   .   .   .

It is not upon the paltry level of negations or of
decent philosophies, it is in the action and hot
mood of creative certitudes that the French battle
is engaged.   The little sophists are dumb and
terrified, their books are quite forgotten.   I myself
forgot (in those few days by that water and in that
city) the thin and ineffectual bodies of ignorant
men who live quite beyond any knowledge of such
fires.   The printed things which tired and poor
writers put down for pay no longer even disturbed
me ; the reflections, the mere phantasms of reality,
with which in a secluded leisure we please our
intellect, faded.   I was like a man who is in the
centre of two lines that meet in war ; to such a
man this fellow's prose on fighting and that one's
verse, this theory of strategy, or that essay upon
arms, are not for one moment remembered.   Here
(in the narrow street which I knew and was now

following) St. Bernard had upheld the sacrament in the shock of the first awakening—in that twelfth century, when Julian stirred in his sleep. Beyond the bridge, in Roman walls that still stand carefully preserved, the Church of Gaul had sustained Athanasius, and determined the course of the Christian centuries. I had passed upon my way the vast and empty room where had been established the Terror; where had been forced by an angry and compelling force the full return of equal laws upon Europe. Who could remember in such an air the follies and the pottering of men who analyse and put in categories and explain the follies of wealth and of old age?

Good Lord, how little the academies became! I remembered the phrases upon one side and upon the other which still live in the stones of the city, carved and deep, but more lasting than are even the letters of their inscription. I remembered the defiant sentence of Mad Dolet on his statue there in the Quarter, the deliberate perversion of Plato, "And when you are dead you shall no more be anything at all." I remembered the "Ave Crux spes Unica"; and St. Just's "The words that we have spoken will never be lost on earth"; and Danton's "Continual Daring," and the scribbled Greek on the walls of the cathedral towers. For not only are the air and the voice, but the very material of this town is filled with words that remain. Certainly the philosophies and the negations dwindled to be so small as at last to disappear, and to leave only the two antagonists.   Passion brooded over the silence of the morning ; there was great energy in the cool of the spring air, and up above, the forms the clouds were taking were forms of gigantic powers.

I came, as the traveller had come, into the cathedral.   It was not yet within half an hour of the feast.   There was still room to be found, though with every moment the nave and the aisles grew fuller, until one doubted how at the end so great a throng could be dismissed.   They were of all kinds.   Some few were strangers holding in their hands books about the building. Some few were devout men on travel, and praying at this great office on the way : men from the islands, men from the places that Spain has re-deemed for the future in the new world.   I saw an Irishman near me, and two West Indians also, half negro, like the third of the kings that came to worship at the manger where Our Lord was born.   For two hours and nearly three I saw and wondered at that immense concourse.   The tri-bunes were full, the whole choir was black, mov-ing with the celebrants, and all the church floor beyond and around me was covered and dark with expectant men.

The Bourdon that had summoned the traveller

and driven mad so many despairs, sounded above
me upon this day with amplitude and yet with
menace.   The silence was a solace when it ceased
to boom.   The Creed, the oldest of our chaunts,
filled and completed those walls ; it was as though
at last a battle had been joined, and in that issue
a great relief ran through the crowd.

.   .   .   .   .   .

From such a temple I came out at last.   They
had thrown the western doors wide open, the doors
whose hinges man scarcely could have hammered
and to whose miracle legend has lent its aid ; the
midday, now captured by the sun, came right into
the hollow simplicity of the nave, and caught the
river of people as they flowed outwards; but even
that and the cry of the Benediction from the altar
gave no greater peace than an appeal to combat.
In the air outside that other power stood waiting
to conquer or to fail.

I came out, as from a camp, into the civilian
debate, the atmosphere of the spectators.   The
permanent and toppling influence against which
this bulwark of ours, the Faith, was reared (as we
say) by God Himself, shouted in half the prints, in
half the houses.   I sat down to read and compare
(as it should be one's custom when one is among
real and determining things) the writings of the
extreme, that is of the leading men.   I chose the

two pamphleteers who are of equal weight in this war, but of whom one only is known as yet to us in England, and that the least.

I read their battle-cries. Their style was excellent; their good faith shone even in their style.

Since I had been upon phrases all these hours I separated and remembered the principal words of each. One said : " They will break their teeth against it. The Catholic Church is not to perish, for she has allies from outside Time." The other said : " How long will the death of this crucified god linger ? How long will his agony crush men with its despair ? "

But I read these two writers for my entertainment only, and in order to be acquainted with men around me ; for on the quarrel between them I had long ago made up my mind.

AT THE SIGN OF THE LION

I T was late, and the day was already falling when I came, sitting my horse Monster, to a rise of land. We were at a walk, for we had gone very far since early morning, and were now off the turf upon the hard road ; moreover, the hill, though gentle, had been prolonged. From its summit I saw before me, as I had seen it a hundred times, the whole of the weald.

But now that landscape was transfigured, because many influences had met to make it, for the moment, an enchanted land. The autumn, coming late, had crowded it with colours ; a slight mist drew out the distances, and along the horizon stood out, quite even and grey like mountains, the solemn presence of the Downs. Over all this the sky was full of storm.

In some manner which language cannot express, and hardly music, the vision was unearthly. All the lesser heights of the plain ministered to one effect, a picture which was to other pictures what the marvellous is to the experience of common things. The distant mills, the edges of heath and the pine trees, were as though they had not before been caught by the eyes of travellers, and would not, after the brief space of their apparition, be seen again. Here was a countryside whose every outline was familiar; and yet it was pervaded by a general quality of the uplifted and the strange. And for that one hour under the sunset the county did not seem to me a thing well known, but rather adored.

The glow of evening, which had seemed to put this horizon into another place and time than ours, warned me of darkness; and I made off the road to the right for an inn I knew of, that stands close to the upper Arun and is very good. Here an old man and his wife live easily, and have so lived for at least thirty years, proving how accessible is content. Their children are in service beyond the boundaries of the county, and are thus provided with sufficiency; and they themselves, the old people, enjoy a small possession which at least does not diminish, for, thank God, their land is free. It is a square of pasture bordered by great elms upon three sides of it, but on the fourth, towards the water, a line of pollard willows; and off a little way before the house runs Arun, sliding as smooth as Mincius, and still so young that he can remember the lake in the forest where he rose.

On such ancestral land these two people await without anxiety what they believe will be a kindly death. Nor is their piety of that violent and tortured kind which is associated with fear and with distress of earlier life ; but they remain peasants, drawing from the earth they have always known as much sustenance for the soul as even their religion can afford them, and mixing that religion so intimately with their experience of the soil that, were they not isolated in an evil time, they would have set up some shrine about the place to sanctify it.

The passion and the strain which must accompany (even in the happiest and most secluded) the working years of life, have so far disappeared from them, that now they can no longer recall any circumstances other than those which they enjoy ; so that their presence in a room about one, as they set food before one or meet one at the door, is in itself an influence of peace.

In such a place, and with such hosts to serve him, the wears of the world retire for a little time, from an evening to a morning ; and a man can enjoy a great refreshment. In such a place he will eat strongly and drink largely, and sleep well and deeply, and, when he saddles again for his journey, he will take the whole world new ; nor are those intervals without their future value, for the memory of a complete repose is a sort of sacrament, and a viaticum for the weary lengths of the way.

The stable of this place is made of oak entirely, and, after more than a hundred years, the wood-work is still sound, save that the roof now falls in waves where the great beams have sagged a little under the pressure of the tiles. And these tiles are of that old hand-made kind which, whenever you find them, you will do well to buy; for they have a slight downward curve to them, and so they fit closer and shed the rain better than if they were flat. Also they do not slip, and thus they put less strain upon the timber. This excellent stable has no flooring but a packed layer of chalk laid on the ground; and the wooden manger is all polished and shining, where it has been rubbed by the noses of ten thousand horses since the great war. That polishing was helped, perhaps, by the nose of Percy's horse, and perhaps by the nose of some wheeler who in his time had dragged the guns back aboard, retreating through the night after Corunna. It is in every way a stable that a small peasant should put up for himself, without seeking money from other men. It is, therefore, a stable which your gaping scientists would condemn; and though as yet they have not got their ugly hands upon the dwellings of beasts as they have upon those of men, yet I often fear for this stable, and am always glad when I come back and find it there. For the men who make our laws are the same as those that sell us our bricks and our land and our metals; and they make the laws so that rebuilding shall go on: and vile rebuilding too.

Anyhow, this stable yet stands; and in none does the horse, Monster, take a greater delight, for he also is open to the influence of holiness. So I led him in, and tied him by the ancient headstall, and I rubbed him down, and I washed his feet and covered him with the rough rug that lay there. And when I had done all that, I got him oats from the neighbouring bin; for the place knew me well, and I could always tend to my own beast when I came there. And as he ate his oats, I said to him: "Monster, my horse, is there any place on earth where a man, even for a little time, can be as happy as the brutes? If there is, it is here at the Sign of The Lion." And Monster answered: "There is a tradition among us that, of all creatures that creep upon the earth, man is the fullest of sorrow."

I left him then, and went towards the house. It was quite dark, and the windows, with their square, large panes and true proportions, shone out and made it home. The room within received me like a friend. The open chimney at its end, round which the house is built, was filled with beech logs burning; and the candles, which were set in brass, mixed their yellow light with that of the fire. The long ceiling was low, as are the

ceilings of Heaven. And oak was here everywhere also : in the beams and the shelves and the
mighty table. For oak was, and will be again,
the chief wood of the weald.

When they put food and ale before me, it was
of the kind which has been English ever since
England began, and which perhaps good fortune
will preserve over the breakdown of our generation, until we have England back again. One
could see the hops in the tankard, and one could
taste the barley, until, more and more sunk into
the plenitude of this good house, one could dare
to contemplate, as though from a distant standpoint, the corruption and the imminent danger of
the time through which we must lead our lives.
And, as I so considered the ruin of the great
cities and their slime, I felt as though I were in
a sort of fortress of virtue and of health, which
could hold out through the pressure of the war.
And I thought to myself : " Perhaps even before
our children are men, these parts which survive
from a better order will be accepted as models,
and England will be built again."

This fantasy had not time, tenuous as it was,
to disappear, before there came into that room a
man whose gesture and bearing promised him to
be an excellent companion, but in whose eyes
I also perceived some light not ordinary. He
was of middle age, fifty or more ; his hair was

crisp and grey, his face brown, as though he had been much upon the sea. He was tall in stature, and of some strength. He saluted me, and, when he had eaten, asked me if I also were familiar with this inn.

"Very familiar," I said; "and since I can enter it at any hour freely, it is now more familiar to me even than the houses that were once my homes. For nowadays we, we who work in the State and are not idle, must be driven from one place to another; and only the very rich have certitude and continuity. But to them it is of no service; for they are too idle to take root in the soil."

"Yet I was of their blood," he said; "and there is in this county a home which should be mine. But nothing to-day is capable of endurance. I have not seen my home (though it is but ten miles from here) since I left it in my thirtieth year; and I too would rather come to this inn, which I know as you know it, than to any house in England; because I am certain of entry, and because I know what I shall find, and because what I find is what any man of this county should find, if the soul of it is not to disappear."

"You, then," I answered (we were now seated side by side before the fire with but one flickering candle behind us, and on the floor between us a port just younger than the host), "you, then, come here for much the same reason as do I?"

"And what is that?" said he.

"Why," said I, "to enjoy the illusion that
Change can somewhere be arrested, and that, in
some shape, a part at least of the things we love
remains. For, since I was a boy and almost since
I can remember, everything in this house has been
the same; and here I escape from the threats of
the society we know."

When I had said this, he was grave and silent
for a little while; and then he answered:

"It is impossible, I think, after many years to
recover any such illusion. Just as a young man
can no longer think himself (as children do) the
actor in any drama of his own choosing, so a man
growing old (as am I) can no longer expect of any
society—and least of all of his own—the gladness
that comes from an illusion of permanence."

"For my part," I answered in turn, "I know
very well, though I can conjure up this feeling of
security, that it is very flimsy stuff; and I take it
rather as men take symbols. For though these
good people will at last perish, and some brewer—
a Colonel of Volunteers as like as not—will buy
this little field, and though for the port we are
drinking there will be imperial port, and for the
beer we have just drunk something as noisome as
that port, and though thistles will grow up in the
good pasture ground, and though, in a word, this
inn will become a hotel and will perish, neverthe-

less I cannot but believe that England remains, and I do not think it the taking of a drug or a deliberate cheating of oneself to come and steep one's soul in what has already endured so long because it was proper to our country."

"All that you say," he answered, "is but part of the attempt to escape Necessity. Your very frame is of that substance for which permanence means death; and every one of all the emotions that you know is of its nature momentary, and must be so if it is to be alive.

"Yet there is a divine thirst," I said, "for something that will not so perish. If there were no such thirst, why should you and I debate such things, or come here to The Lion either of us, to taste antiquity? And if that thirst is there, it is a proof that there is for us some End and some such satisfaction. For my part, as I know of nothing else, I cannot but seek it in this visible good world. I seek it in Sussex, in the nature of my home, and in the tradition of my blood."

But he answered: "No; it is not thus to be attained, the end of which you speak. And that thirst, which surely is divine, is to be quenched in no stream that we can find by journeying, not even in the little rivers that run here under the combes of home."

MYSELF: "Well, then, what is the End?"

HE: "I have sometimes seen it clearly, that

when the disappointed quest was over, all this journeying would turn out to be but the beginning of a much greater adventure, and that I should set out towards another place where every sense should be fulfilled, and where the fear of mutation should be set at rest."

MYSELF: " No one denies that such a picture in the mind haunts men their whole lives through, though, after they have once experienced loss and incompletion, and especially when they have caught sight a long way off of the Barrier which ends all our experience, they recognize that picture for a cheat ; and surely nothing can save it ? That which reasons in us may be absolute and undying; for it is outside Time.   It escapes the gropings of the learned, and it has nothing to do with material things.   But as for all those functions which we but half fulfil in life, surely elsewhere they cannot be fulfilled at all ? Colour is for the eyes and music is for the ears ; and all that we love so much comes in by channels that do not remain."

HE : " Yet the Desire can only be for things that we have known ; and the Desire, as you have said, is a proof of the thing desired, and, but for these things which we know, the words ' joy ' and ' contentment ' and ' fulfilment ' would have no meaning."

MYSELF: " Why yes ; but, though desires are the strongest evidence of truth, yet there is also desire for illusions, as there is a waking demand for things attainable, and a demand in dreams for things fantastic and unreal. Every analogy increasingly persuades us, and so does the whole scheme of things as we learn it, that, with our passing, there shall also pass speech and comfortable fires and fields and the voices of our children, and that, when they pass, we lose them for ever."

HE: "Yet these things would not be, but for the mind which receives them; and how can we make sure what channels are necessary for the mind? and may not the mind stretch on? And you, since you reject my guess at what may be reserved for us, tell me, what is the End which we shall attain?"

MYSELF: "*Salva fide*, I cannot tell."

Then he continued and said: "I have too long considered these matters for any opposition between one experience and another to affect my spirit, and I know that a long and careful inquiry into any matter must lead the same man to opposing conclusions; but, for my part, I shall confidently expect throughout that old age, which is not far from me, that, when it ceases, I shall find beyond it things similar to those which I have known. For all I here enjoy is of one nature; and if the life of a man be bereft of them at last, then it is falsehood or metaphor to use the word 'eternal.'"

" You think, then," said I, "that some immortal part in us is concerned not only with our knowledge, but with our every feeling, and that our final satisfaction will include a sensual pleasure: fragrance, and landscape, and a visible home that shall be dearer even than are these dear hills?"

"Something of the sort," he said, and slightly shrugged his shoulders. They were broad, as he sat beside me staring at the fire. They conveyed in their attitude that effect of mingled strength and weariness which is common to all who have travelled far and with great purpose, perpetually seeking some worthy thing which they could never find.

The fire had fallen. Flames no longer leapt from the beech logs; but on their under side, where a glow still lingered, embers fell.

THE AUTUMN
AND THE FALL OF LEAVES

I T is not true that the close of a life which ends
in a natural fashion—life which is permitted to
put on the pomp of death and to go out in glory—
inclines the mind to repose. It is not true of a day
ending nor the passing of the year, nor of the fall
of leaves. Whatever permanent, uneasy question
is native to men, comes forward most insistent and
most loud at such times.

There is a house in my own county which is
built of stone, whose gardens are fitted to the
autumn. It has level alleys standing high and
banked with stone. Their ornaments were carved
under the influence of that restraint which marked
the Stuarts. They stand above old ponds, and
are strewn at this moment with the leaves of elms.
These walks are like the Mailles of the Flemish
cities, the walls of the French towns or the terraces
of the Loire. They are enjoyed to-day by whoever has seen all our time go racing by ; they are
the proper resting-places of the aged, and their
spirit is felt especially in the fall of leaves.

At this season a sky which is of so delicate and
faint a blue as to contain something of gentle
mockery, and certainly more of tenderness, pre-
sides at the fall of leaves.   There is no air, no
breath at all.   The leaves are so light that they
sidle on their going downward, hesitating in that
which is not void to them, and touching at last so
imperceptibly the earth with which they are to
mingle, that the gesture is much gentler than a
salutation, and even more discreet than a discreet
caress.

They make a little sound, less than the
least of sounds.   No bird at night in the marshes
rustles so slightly ; no men, though men are the
subtlest of living beings, put so evanescent a stress
upon their sacred whispers or their prayers.   The
leaves are hardly heard, but they are heard just so
much that men also, who are destined at the end to
grow glorious and to die, look up and hear them
falling.

    .   .   .   .   .   .

With what a pageantry of every sort is not that
troubling symbol surrounded !   The scent of life
is never fuller in the woods than now, for the
ground is yielding up its memories.   The spring
when it comes will not restore this fullness, nor
these deep and ample recollections of the earth.
For the earth seems now to remember the drive
of the ploughshare and its harrying ; the seed,

and the full bursting of it, the swelling and the completion of the harvest.   Up to the edge of the woods throughout the weald the earth has borne fruit ; the barns are full, and the wheat is standing stacked in the fields, and there are orchards all around.   It is upon such a mood of parentage and of fruition that the dead leaves fall.

Their colour is not a mere splendour : it is intricate.   The same unbounded power, never at fault and never in calculation, which comprehends all the landscape, and which has made the woods, has worked in each one separate leaf as well ; they are inconceivably varied.   Take up one leaf and see.   How many kinds of boundary are there here between the stain which ends in a sharp edge against the gold, and the sweep in which the purple and red mingle more evenly than they do in shot-silk or in flames ?   Nor are the boundaries to be measured only by degrees of definition.   They have also their characters of line.   Here in this leaf are boundaries intermittent, boundaries rugged, boundaries curved, and boundaries broken.   Nor do shape and definition even begin to exhaust the list.   For there are softness and hardness too : the agreement and disagreement with the scheme of veins ; the grotesque and the simple in line ; the sharp and the broad, the smooth, and raised in boundaries.   So in this one matter of boundaries might you discover for ever new things ; there is

no end to them.   Their qualities are infinite.
And beside boundaries you have hues and tints,
shades also, varying thicknesses of stuff, and endless choice of surface; that list also is infinite, and
the divisions of each item in it are infinite; nor is it
of any use to analyse the thing, for everywhere the
depth and the meaning of so much creation are beyond our powers.   And all this is true of but one
dead leaf; and yet every dead leaf will differ from its
fellow.

That which has delighted to excel in boundless-
ness within the bounds of this one leaf, has also
transformed the whole forest.   There is no number
to the particular colours of the one leaf.   This
forest is like a thing so changeful of its nature
that change clings to it as a quality, apparent even
during the glance of a moment.   This forest makes
a picture which is designed, but not seizable.   It
is a scheme, but a scheme you cannot set down.
It is of those things which can best be retained by
mere copying with a pencil or a brush.   It is of
those things which a man cannot fully receive,
and which he cannot fully re-express to other
men.

It is no wonder, then, that at this peculiar time,
this week (or moment) of the year, the desires
which if they do not prove at least demand—perhaps remember—our destiny, come strongest.
They are proper to the time of autumn, and all

men feel them.   The air is at once new and old ;
the morning (if one rises early enough to welcome
its leisurely advance) contains something in it of
profound reminiscence.   The evenings hardly yet
suggest (as they soon will) friends and security,
and the fires of home.   The thoughts awakened in
us by their bands of light fading along the downs
are thoughts which go with loneliness and prepare
me for the isolation of the soul.

It is on this account that tradition has set, at the
entering of autumn, for a watch at the gate of the
season, the Archangel ; and at its close the day
and the night of All-Hallows on which the dead
return.

THE GOOD WOMAN

UPON a hill that overlooks a western plain
and is conspicuous at the approach of evening, there still stands a house of faded brick faced
with cornerings of stone. It is quite empty, but
yet not deserted. In each room some little furni-
ture remains; all the pictures are upon the walls;
the deep red damask of the panels is not faded, or
if faded, shows no contrast of brighter patches, for
nothing has been removed from the walls. Here
it is possible to linger for many hours alone, and
to watch the slope of the hill under the level light
as the sun descends. Here passed a woman of
such nobility that, though she is dead, the landscape and the vines are hers.

It was in September, during a silence of the air,
that I first saw her as she moved among her pos-
sessions; she was smiling to herself as though at
a memory, but her smile was so slight and so dignified, so genial, and yet so restrained, that you
would have thought it part of everything around
and married (as she was) to the land which was
now her own. She wandered down the garden

paths ruling the flowers upon either side, and receiving as she went autumn and the fruition of her fields; plenitude and completion surrounded her; the benediction of Almighty God must have been upon her, for she was the fulfilment of her world.

Three fountains played in that garden—two, next to the northern and the southern walls, were small and low; they rather flowed than rose. Two cones of marble received their fall, and over these they spread in an even sheet with little noise, making (as it were) a sheath of water which covered all the stone; but the third sprang into the air with delicate triumph, fine and high, satisfied, tenous and exultant. This one tossed its summit into the light, and, alone of the things in the garden, the plash of its waters recalled and suggested activity—though that in so discreet a way that it was to be heard rather than regarded. The birds flew far off in circles over the roofs of the town below us. Very soon they went to their rest.

The slow transfiguration of the light by which the air became full of colours and every outline merged into the evening, made of all I saw, as I came up towards her, a soft and united vision wherein her advancing figure stood up central and gave a meaning to the whole. I will not swear that she did not as she came bestow as well as receive an influence of the sunset. It was said by the ancients that virtue is active, an agent, and has power to control created things ; for, they said, it is in a direct relation with whatever orders and has ordained the general scheme. Such power, perhaps, resided in her hands. It would have awed me but hardly astonished if, as the twilight deepened, the inclination of the stems had obeyed her gesture and she had put the place to sleep.

As I came near I saw her plainly. Her face was young although she was so wise, but its youth had the aspect of a divine survival. Time adorned it.

Music survives. Whatever is eternal in the grace of simple airs or in the Christian innocence of Mozart was apparent, nay, had increased, in her features as the days in passing had added to them not only experience but also revelation and security. She was serene. The posture of her head was high, and her body, which was visibly informed by an immortal spirit, had in its carriage a large, a regal, an uplifted bearing which even now as I write of it, after so many years, turns common every other sight that has encountered me. This was the way in which I first saw her upon her own hillside at evening.

With every season I returned. And with every season she greeted my coming with a more generous and a more vivacious air. I think the years slipped off and did not add themselves upon her mind: the common doom of mortality escaped her until, perhaps, its sign was imposed upon her hair—for this at last was touched all through with that appearance or gleam which might be morning or which might be snow.

She was able to conjure all evil. Those desperate enemies of mankind which lie in siege of us all around grew feeble and were silent when she came. Nor has any other force than hers dared to enter the rooms where she had lived: it is her influence alone which inhabits them to-day. There is a vessel of copper, enamelled in green and gilded, which she gave with her own hands to a friend overseas. I have twice touched it in an evil hour.

Strength, sustenance, and a sacramental justice are permanent in such lives, and such lives also attain before their close to so general a survey of the world that their appreciations are at once accurate and universal.

On this account she did not fail in any human conversation, nor was she ever for a moment less than herself; but always and throughout her moods her laughter was unexpected and full, her fear natural, her indignation glorious.

Above all, her charity extended like a breeze: it enveloped everything she knew. The sense of destiny faded from me as the warmth of that charity fell upon my soul; the foreknowledge of

death retreated, as did every other unworthy
panic.

She drew the objects of her friendship into
something new; they breathed an air from another
country, so that those whom she deigned to regard
were, compared with other men, like the living
compared with the dead ; or, better still, they were
like men awake while the rest were tortured by
dreams and haunted of the unreal. Indeed, she
had a word given to her which saved all the souls
of her acquaintance.

It is not true that influence of this sort decays
or passes into vaguer and vaguer depths of mem-
mory. It does not dissipate. It is not dissolved.
It does not only spread and broaden : it also in-
creases with the passage of time. The musicians
bequeath their spirit, notably those who have loved
delightful themes and easy melodies. The poets
are read for ever ; but those who resemble her do
more, for they grow out upon the centuries—they
themselves and not their arts continue. There is
stuff in their legend. They are a tangible inheritance for the hurrying generations of men.

She was of this kind. She was certainly of this
kind. She died upon this day* in the year 1892.
In these lines I perpetuate her memory.

* 22 December.

THE HARBOUR IN THE NORTH

UPON that shore of Europe which looks out towards no further shore, I came once by accident upon a certain man.

The day had been warm and almost calm, but a little breeze from the south-east had all day long given life to the sea. The seas had run very small and brilliant, yet without violence, before the wind, and had broken upon the granite cliffs to leeward, not in spouts of foam, but in a white, even line that was thin, and from which one heard no sound of surge. Moreover, as I was running dead north along the coast, the noise about the bows was very slight and pleasant. The regular and gentle wind came upon the quarter without change, and the heel of the boat was steady. No calm came with the late sunset; the breeze still held, and so till nearly midnight I could hold a course and hardly feel the pulling of the helm. Meanwhile the arch of the sunset endured, for I was far to the northward, and all those colours which belong to June above the Arctic Sea shone and changed in the slow progress of that arch as

307

it advanced before me and mingled at last with
the dawn.   Throughout the hours of that journey
I could see clearly the seams of the deck forward,
the texture of the canvas and the natural hues of
the woodwork and the rigging, the glint of the
brasswork, and even the letters painted round the
little capstan-head, so continually did the light
endure.   The silence which properly belongs to
darkness, and which accompanies the sleep of
birds upon the sea, appeared to be the more
intense because of such a continuance of the
light, and what with a long vigil and new water,
it was as though I had passed the edge of all
known maps and had crossed the boundary of new
land.

In such a mood I saw before me the dark band
of a stone jetty running some miles off from the
shore into the sea, and at the end of it a fixed
beacon whose gleam showed against the translucent sky (and its broken reflection in the pale
sea) as a candle shows when one pulls the curtains
of one's room and lets in the beginnings of the
day.

For this point I ran, and as I turned it I discovered a little harbour quite silent under the
growing light; there was not a man upon its
wharves, and there was no smoke rising from its
slate roofs.   It was absolutely still.   The boat
swung easily round in the calm water, the pier-

head slipped by, the screen of the pier-head beacon suddenly cut off its glare, and she went slowly with no air in her canvas towards the patch of darkness under the quay. There, as I did not know the place, I would not pick up moorings which another man might own and need, but as my boat still crept along with what was left of her way I let go the little anchor, for it was within an hour of low tide, and I was sure of water.

When I had done this she soon tugged at the chain and I slackened all the halyards. I put the cover on the mainsail, and as I did so, looking aft, I noted the high mountain-side behind the town standing clear in the dawn. I turned eastward to receive it. The light still lifted, and though I had not slept I could not but stay up and watch the glory growing over heaven. It was just then, when I had stowed everything away, that I heard to the right of me the crooning of a man.

A few moments before I should not have seen him under the darkness of the sea-wall, but the light was so largely advanced (it was nearly two o'clock) that I now clearly made out both his craft and him.

She was sturdy and high, and I should think of slight draught. She was of great beam. She carried but one sail, and that was brown. He had it loose, with the peak dipped ready for hoisting, and he himself was busy at some work upon her floor, stowing and fitting his bundles, and as he worked he crooned gently to himself It was then that I hailed him, but in a low voice, so much did the silence of that place impress itself upon all living beings who were strange to it. He looked up and told me that he had not seen me come in nor heard the rattling of the chain. I asked him what he would do so early, whether he was off fishing at that hour or whether he was taking parcels down the coast for hire or goods to sell at some other port. He answered me that he was doing none of those things.

" What cruise, then, are you about to take?" I said.

"I am off," he answered in a low and happy voice, "to find what is beyond the sea."

"And to what shore," said I, "do you mean to sail?"

He answered: "I am out upon this sea northward to where they say there is no further shore."

As he spoke he looked towards that horizon which now stood quite clean and clear between the pier-heads: his eyes were full of the broad daylight, and he breathed the rising wind as though it were a promise of new life and of unexpected things. I asked him then what his security was and had he formed a plan, and why he was setting out from this small place, unless, perhaps, it was his home, of which he might be tired.

"No," he answered, and smiled; "this is not my home; and I have come to it as you may have come to it, for the first time; and, like you, I came in after the whole place slept; but as I neared I noticed certain shoremarks and signs which had been given me, and then I knew that I had come to the starting-place of a long voyage."

"Of what voyage?" I asked.

He answered:

"This is that harbour in the North of which a Breton priest once told me that I should reach it, and when I had moored in it and laid my stores on board in order, I should set sail before morning and reach at last a complete repose." Then he went on with eagerness, though still talking low: "The voyage which I was born to make in the end, and to which my desire has driven me, is towards a place in which everything we have known is forgotten, except those things which, as we knew them, reminded us of an original joy. In that place I shall discover again such full moments of content as I have known, and I shall preserve them without failing. It is in some country beyond this sea, and it has a harbour like this harbour, only set towards the South, as this is towards the North; but like this harbour it looks out over an unknown sea, and like this harbour it enjoys a perpetual light. Of what the happy people in this country are, or of how they speak, no one has told me, but they will receive me well, for I am of one kind with themselves. But as to how I shall know this harbour, I can tell you : there is a range of hills, broken by a valley through which one sees a further and a higher range, and steering for this hollow in the hills one sees a tower out to sea upon a rock, and high up inland a white quarry on a hill-top ; and these two in line are the leading marks by which one gets clear into the mouth of the river, and so to the wharves of the town.   And there," he ended, " I shall come off the sea for ever, and every one will call me by my name."

The sun was now near the horizon, but not yet risen, and for a little time he said nothing to me nor I to him, for he was at work sweating up the halyard and setting the peak. He let go the mooring knot also, but he held the end of the rope in his hand and paid it out, standing and looking upward, as the sail slowly filled and his craft drifted towards me. He pressed the tiller with his knee to keep her full.

I now knew by his eyes and voice that he was from the West, and I could not see him leave me without asking him from what place he came that he should set out for such another place. So I asked him : "Are you from Ireland, or from Brittany, or from the Islands ? " He answered me : " I am from none of these, but from Cornwall."

And as he answered me thus shortly he still watched the sail and still pressed the tiller with his knee, and still paid out the mooring rope without turning round.

"You cannot make the harbour," I said to him. "It is not of this world."

Just at that moment the breeze caught the peak of his jolly brown sail; he dropped the tail of the rope: it slipped and splashed into the harbour slime. His large boat heeled, shot up, just missed my cable; and then he let her go free, and she ran clear away. As she ran he looked over his shoulder and laughed most cheerily; he greeted me with his eyes, and he waved his hand to me in the morning light.

He held her well. A clean wake ran behind her. He put her straight for the harbour-mouth and passed the pier-heads and took the sea outside.

Whether in honest truth he was a fisherman out for fishes who chose to fence with me, or whether in that cruise of his he landed up in a Norwegian bay, or thought better of it in Orkney, or went through the sea and through death to the place he desired, I have never known.

I watched him holding on, and certainly he kept a course. The sun rose, the town awoke, but I would not cease from watching him. His sail still showed a smaller and a smaller point upon the sea; he did not waver. For an hour I caught it and lost it, and caught it again, as it dwindled ; for half another hour I could not swear to it in the blaze.   Before I had wearied it was gone.

.   .   .   .   .   .

Oh ! my companions, both you to whom I dedicate this book and you who have accompanied me over other hills and across other waters or before the guns in Burgundy, or you others who were with me when I seemed alone—that ulterior shore was the place we were seeking in every cruise and march and the place we thought at last to see. We, too, had in mind that Town of which this man spoke to me in the Scottish harbour before he sailed out northward to find what he could find.   But I did not follow him, for even if I had followed him I should not have found the Town.